Learning and Study Skills Program Level 1

Teacher's Guide

Third Edition

Developed by:	The Study Skills Group
Author:	Candace Regan Burkle
Co-Author and Editor:	David Marshak
Editorial Board:	Kiyo Morimoto, former *Director* Bureau of Study Counsel Harvard University Jerome A. Peih, *Headmaster,* Milton Academy

ScarecrowEducation
Lanham, Maryland • Toronto • Oxford

Published in the United States of America
by ScarecrowEducation
An imprint of The Rowman & Littlefield Publishing Group, Inc.
4501 Forbes Boulevard, Suite 200, Lanham, Maryland 20706
www.scarecroweducation.com

PO Box 317
Oxford
OX2 9RU, UK

Our thanks to all the hundreds of teachers, students, counselors, and administrators who used the first and second editions of LEVEL I PROGRAM and contributed their suggestions to us.

Resources reviewed by Kathy Barwin. Illustrations by Joe Bolger.

British Library Cataloguing in Publication Information Available

Library of Congress Cataloging-in-Publication Data

ISBN 0-8108-4641-1

♾™ The paper used in this publication meets the minimum requirements of American National Standard for Information Sciences—Permanence of Paper for Printed Library Materials, ANSI/NISO Z39.48-1992. Manufactured in the United States of America.

TABLE OF CONTENTS

Introduction to the *hm Learning and Study Skills Program: Level I* 1

INTRODUCTION TO LEARNING AND STUDY SKILLS 12

UNIT I: WAYS TO LISTEN 17

UNIT II: TUNING INTO DIRECTIONS 38

UNIT III: GETTING THE TIMING DOWN 52

UNIT IV: A MATTER OF TIME 72

UNIT V: PUTTING IDEAS TOGETHER 92

UNIT VI: PICTURING IN YOUR MIND'S EYE 115

UNIT VII: READING FOR MEANING 139

UNIT VIII: TAKING NOTES — MAPPING AND OUTLINING 166

UNIT IX: LISTENING AND TAKING NOTES 177

UNIT X: IMPROVING YOUR VOCABULARY 187

UNIT XI: ORGANIZING IDEAS 198

UNIT XII: CHARTS — TABLES AND GRAPHS 212

UNIT XIII: USING A DICTIONARY 236

UNIT XIV: PUTTING A BOOK TOGETHER 249

UNIT XV: STUDYING AND TEST TAKING 266

INTRODUCTION TO THE hm
LEARNING AND STUDY SKILLS PROGRAM: LEVEL I

Dear Colleague:

The *hm* **Learning and Study Skills Program: Level I** is designed to provide you with a valuable resource for the teaching of learning and study skills. Please read this Introduction carefully so you can gain a sense of the purposes and values, the means and ends, and the capacities and limitations of this **Program**.

Please note that this is the **third edition** of the *hm* **Learning and Study Skills Program: Level I**.

LEARNING AND STUDY SKILLS: WHAT ARE THEY?

Learning and study skills are methods for acquiring knowledge, understanding, and competence. A look at the listing of units in this **Program** will give you examples of important learning and study skills, such as listening, taking notes, and organizing ideas.

In the literal sense, study skills involve specific, observable behaviors that can be described and measured. For example, can a student attend to a set of directions and follow them accurately? Can a student plan the use of his or her study time and follow that schedule? Can a student take useful notes from an oral presentation? Can a student read a section of text and identify the main ideas and important details?

There is also a more profound definition of learning and study skills than this literal one. In this larger sense, learning and study skills are processes for learning. They are processes that help students to organize and direct the effort they invest in learning, and their use results in students becoming more effective and efficient learners who are more in charge of their own learning. When students master a skill for learning, they are learning more than just a technique. They are learning a way of solving learning problems, a method of approach and follow-through that can be used in any relevant context. They are also learning more about how to learn effectively. It is this larger understanding of study skills that reveals their central role in schooling.

1

LEARNING SKILLS AND STUDY SKILLS: WHAT'S THE DIFFERENCE?

Many educators equate the terms *learning skills* and *study skills*. Others see a shade of sifference in their meanings, with study skills referring primarily to school-based learning and learning skills referring to learning in any context. In this third edition of the **hm Learning and Study Skills Program: Level I**, we have chosen to join these terms together so that we can emphasize our belief that the skills for learning are essential in every learning context: in school, at home, in post-secondary education, and in the workplace.

As we re-invent our schools for the needs of our students in the 21st century, we are coming to understand that students must be active, meaning-seeking and meaning-making learners. Learning and study skills are among the tools that students need to be able to use well as they engage in their meaning-seeking and meaning-making activities.

THE hm LEARNING AND STUDY SKILLS PROGRAM: LEVEL I

The *hm* **Learning and Study Skills Program: Level** I is designed to provide *an introduction to learning and study skills* for 5th, 6th, and 7th grade students through a series of fifteen activity-oriented units. Some of the units can be completed in one period of class time. Others will require more than a single period.

The *hm* **Program** is structured on the assumption that activity-oriented lessons are the most effective instructional strategy for the teaching of learning and study skills: more succinctly, that "learning by doing" is the best way to master learning and study skills.

The *hm* **Study Skills Program: Level** I is *not* remedial in character. Rather, it is designed to assist students at most levels of competence in their development of essential learning and study skills, and to reinforce already existing skills.

The **Program** is deliberately designed to address a wide range of student needs:

1. For the student who has little sense of a particular skill, it provides an introduction to the skill.

2. For the student who is ready to acquire initial competence in a skill, it provides a learning experience.

3. For the student who has already mastered a skill, participation in one of the **Program's** lessons offers review, reinforcement, and the opportunity to increase one's level of competence in that skill.

Thus, the **Program** allows for the participation of students with a wide range of skills and promotes learning on various levels of competence.

The *hm* **Learning and Study Skills Program: Level I** can serve as a workbook for classroom use. After the completion of the last unit, students should be allowed to keep their **Program,** so the **Program** can be a resource and handbook to which they can refer throughout the same school year and subsequent ones. Or, **Programs** may be reused as needed.

THE DEVELOPMENTAL CHARACTER OF THE
hm LEARNING AND STUDY SKILLS PROGRAM: LEVEL I

The *hm* **Learning and Study Skills Program: Level I** is based on a developmental understanding of the capacities and needs of 5th, 6th, and 7th graders. Young people of these ages still learn effectively through interaction with materials, but many of them are also beginning to develop the capacity for abstraction.

The study skills presented in this **Program** are particularly appropriate for young people of these ages. Some of these skills help students to use their capacities to listen, visualize, and focus their attention more effectively. Other learning and study skills help young people to develop their competence in more analytic and abstract areas such as following directions, sequencing, note taking, reading for meaning, and studying.

STUDY SKILLS AND LEARNING STYLE

Research in cognitive and learning styles during the past three decades has demonstrated what perceptive classroom teachers have known for a long time: people learn in very different and personal ways. Thus, learning and study skills should not be taught in a rigid and prescriptive manner that indicates to students that all individuals ought to develop exactly the same repertoire of skills. Rather, as is appropriate to their level of maturity, students need to be involved in a self-reflective process whereby they learn more about their own learning styles while they are learning specific learning and study skills. Instruction that is guided by an awareness of individual differences in learning style will help students to develop learning and study skills that are specifically useful to their capacities, needs, and desires.

The **hm Learning and Study Skills Program: Level I** is grounded in an awareness of the importance of learning style as a powerful factor in all learning, including the learning of study skills. The **Program** introduces the concept of learning style to students in the "Introduction" and raises learning style issues as is appropriate throughout its fifteen units.

USING THE hm LEARNING AND STUDY SKILLS PROGRAM: LEVEL I

WHEN TO TEACH THE hm PROGRAM: LEVEL I

Classroom use of the *hm* **Program: Level I** has demonstrated that the activities in this **Program** are appropriate for 5th, 6th, and 7th graders.

You may also find the **Program** to be of value with some students who are in classes above 7th grade.

SEQUENCE OF INSTRUCTION

We have sequenced the fifteen units in the **Program** in an order that is developmentally sound and effectively balanced in terms of the diversity of the activities within the various units. You may want to teach the units in this order. However, you may find that it is preferable for your students' needs to generate your own order of instruction. If you do so, you'll want to be aware of the connections among the various units and use these connections effectively in your instruction. For example, Units VII, VIII, and IX are directly connected, forming a coherent sequence of instruction.

WHERE TO TEACH THE hm STUDY SKILLS PROGRAM

The learning and study skills included in the *hm* **Learning and Study Skills Program: Level I** are ones that are useful in the study of almost every subject. Thus, the **Program** can be successfully taught within the context of any subject with the exception, perhaps, of mathematics. (The *hm* **Math Learning and Study Skills Program** provides a learning and study skills resource for the mathematics classroom.) We have observed the effective use of previous editions of this **Program** in social studies, English, science, and reading classes. We have also seen parts of it put to good use in home economics, foreign language, industrial arts and vocational training, and even physical education classes.

BUILDING LEARNING AND STUDY SKILLS INSTRUCTION INTO THE CURRICULUM

We strongly recommend that you teach the units from the *hm* **Learning and Study Skills Program** within the context of an already existing course or class rather than in a mini-course or homeroom setting. Only in the regular classroom can the teacher of the *hm* **Program** integrate study skills with the curriculum of her or his course and help the student to see both the immediate and long-term value of mastering and employing study skills.

Be aware that each unit offers an introduction to the learning and study skill(s) to be studied and practiced. Most students will need to study and practice each skill(s) over time to achieve competence in using the skill(s).

PACING OF THE hm PROGRAM

Our evaluation of the classroom use of the previous editions of this **Program** has informed us that there is no single pacing for the teaching of the units that we can recommend. Rather, we have learned that teachers must decide for themselves how to pace these units in a way that helps students to learn and begin to master the various study skills.

Some of the pacings that have been used effectively by classroom teachers include:

a. A division of the instructional responsibility for the units in the **Program** among different subject area teachers, with each one teaching some part of the **Program**;

b. Three or four units in a one month period; then, a second month for ongoing practice of these skills, followed by the use of another three or four units in a one month period; and so on;

c. One unit every 3-4 weeks over the length of most of the school year;

d. A focus on 4-6 of these learning and study skills in 5th grade, another 4-6 in 6th grade, and the remaining learning and study skills in 7th grade.

We suggest that you adopt an instructional strategy for learning and study skills that is suited to the needs of your students. We strongly recommend that you design a strategy that will provide opportunity for the immediate application and reinforcement of the various learning and study skills that students can learn through this **Program.**

PREPARING YOUR STUDENTS

Your students will approach a unit with more direction, confidence, and enthusiasm if you begin the unit by giving them an overview of what they are going to learn. You can usually fmd one or two key ideas in the unit introduction in the **Teacher's Guide** that will help you do this. You can also find these key ideas in the Unit Summaries.

SUGGESTED DIRECTIONS

The **Teacher's Guide** offers suggested directions for teaching each unit in the **Program.** Our classroom testing has shown these methods to be useful. Of course, we invite you to adapt them in ways that are most appropriate for your students and your own teaching style.

We suggest that you examine both the **Student Text** and the **Teacher's Guide** caref prior to teaching each unit.

THE CONTENT INCLUDED IN THIS PROGRAM IS COMPLETE WITH TWO EXCEPTIONS:

Unit IX calls upon you to create and deliver a short talk and to structure and lead a brief class discussion. See pages 177-186 in the **Teacher's Guide.**

SUGGESTED TIMES

Each section of the suggested directions in the **Teacher's Guide** includes approximate times for the activities within that section. These estimates will help you plan individual lessons or instructional periods. Unit time estimates range from 40-120 minutes. Our field test has demonstrated that 30-40 minutes of working with learning and study skills is a productive amount of time. Thus you will probably need to plan for several blocks of time or class periods to complete the activities in many of the units.

Our classroom testing experience has also shown us that wide variation in teaching style and student levels results in an equally wide variation in the instructional time needed for any one exercise. We suggest that you examine the **Program's** units carefully and gauge your planning of instructional time according to your knowledge of how things actually work in your classroom.

UNIT SUMMARIES

Each unit includes a summary as its final section. While the use of the summaries has not been formally integrated into the suggested directions, many teachers have found that the precise wording of these summaries helped students understand what they were learning and why.

ADDITIONAL SUGGESTIONS

Additional Suggestions for each unit are provided in the **Teacher's Guide.** These suggestions are ideas and activities that build on the skills and concepts introduced in the units. These suggestions provide opportunities for additional practice of the learning and study skill(s) and demonstrate a variety of applications of each new skill. We recommend that you read through the Additional Suggestions prior to teaching a unit. This will give you a better sense of the purpose and direction of the unit.

We suggest that you plan to use some of the relevant suggested activities in the days following your teaching of each of the **Program's** units. You'll want to keep others in mind for use later in the year.

ADDITIONAL SUGGESTIONS AND RECOMMENDATIONS

USING SMALL GROUPS IN THE CLASSROOM

For some of the activities in the **hm Program,** we have recommended organizing your students into small working groups. We have done this for the following reasons:

(1)   Small group processes genuinely engage students in an activity.

(2)   Students can share their talents and experience and learn from each other.

(3)   Because they offer active participation to each and every student, such processes help both to enhance motivation for learning and increase interest in the content of a lesson.

You may wish to select the membership of the small groups for each exercise based upon your knowledge of your students. Some teachers have found it valuable to maintain fixed groups for periods of time to offer students the experience of developing positive and efficient working relationships.

Individual work is also of critical importance to the learning of learning and study skills. When a skill has been introduced in a group setting, it is necessary to provide for individual work with that skill through other activities.

STUDENT DISCUSSION

Students need the opportunity to discuss their work if they are to learn study and learning skills effectively and know how and when to use them. Their discussion must include not only the "right answer" (if there is one) but also the process through which they arrived at the answer and their reasons for considering it correct. At this point in your student's development of learning and study skills, *the process is more important than the individual answer.* For these reasons, we have included oral activities and the opportunity for small and large group discussion throughout the **Program**.

LEARNING STUDY SKILLS: TRIAL AND ERROR

People learn skills through processes of repeated trial and error. One key to learning and study skills teaching, then, is providing students with sufficient opportunity for practice of the skill to be learned. The **hm Study Skills Program: Level I** includes only a few practices of each skill that it introduces. If your students are to master the learning and study skills presented by the **Program**, it is essential that you provide them with structured and ongoing opportunities for practice of the various skills. For example, we know of teachers who have selected four or five learning and study skills that they judged to be of the greatest value in their classes and have focused their instruction on these in the weeks and months after their initial use of the entire **Program**.

Of course, there is an inevitable tension between providing your students with trial and error practice of a new learning skill and helping your students to maintain their interest in mastering the skill in the face of the necessary repetition. While this tension cannot be willed away, we are confident that you can minimize it by using variation and imagination in your instructional design. For example, if your students are learning to take notes, let them practice their skills in a wide variety of contexts and for many different purposes. Also, as your students practice a new learning and study skill, help them to see the benefits that they will gain from their increasing mastery of the skill.

LEARNING STUDY SKILLS: LEARNING FROM ERRORS

An important key to teaching learning and study skills is the recognition that learning a new skill requires most learners to err before they can succeed. We learn skills by being presented with a new skill, trying to use that skill ourselves, committing errors, identifying our errors and then correcting them. Understanding this process creates several responsibilities for the teacher:

(a)   The teacher must encourage students to ask questions when they do not understand an idea or directive. Knowing when to ask questions is an important characteristic of the effective learner.

(b)   The teacher must provide a space within the learning process where students can try out a new skill, make errors, but not feel that they have failed or are "failures."

(c)   The teacher must provide students with enough opportunities for practice of the new skill so that students begin to master the skill and see its usefulness.

(d)   The teacher must provide usable feedback to students about the effectiveness of their use of the new learning skill so that they understand that they can now do certain things that they could not do before.

(e)   The teacher must reward students for what they have done well in using the new skill. With such recognition, students experience success in the learning process, validated both by their own new ability and by the teacher's recognition of this. The experience of success motivates students to continue the development of mastery of the new learning skill.

GRADING AND THE hm STUDY SKILLS PROGRAM

Given the grade-oriented reality of most schools, we suggest that students' involvement with the *hm* **Program** be graded in some fair and concrete manner. We propose a standards-based approach for this grading, which is informed by the process of how skills are learned—through repeated practice over time—and which sets reasonable levels of expected competence. With standards-based grading, students' grades result not from each practice with the skill but from the level of competence that students achieve in that skill at the end of a certain amount of time.

We also suggest that you inform your students about how their work with the hm **Program** will be evaluated at the very beginning of their use of the **Program.**

ADDITIONAL COMMENTS

The *hm* **Study Skills Program** is designed to be taught by a teacher in a classroom setting. It is not programmed material that students can work through by themselves, although some of the units can be used on an individual basis.

The *hm* **Study Skills Program** incorporates as much student activity as possible, including individual, small group, and whole class activities. This emphasis results from our conviction that people learn skills best by doing.

It's important to note that the *hm* **Program** can also serve as a diagnostic tool for your use. An inspection of your students' working of the various units will provide you with specific information about their learning and study skills competencies. It will show you clearly what they already know and on what you need to focus your instructional attention.

We strongly recommend that you provide your students with an overview concerning the values and purposes of learning and study skills both in your classroom and throughout their lives.

OTHER hm STUDY SKILLS PROGRAMS

The hm Study Skills Program: Level A..for grades 1-2
The hm Study Skills Program: Level B..for grades 3-4
The hm Math Learning and Study Skills Program..for grades 6-10
The hm Science Learning and Study Skills Program..for grades 7-10
The hm Learning and Study Skills Program: Level II...for grades 8-10
The hm Learning and Study Skills Program: Level III..for grades 11-13
The hm Study Skills Inventory 1...for grades 4-7
The hm Study Skills Inventory 2... for grades 8-12

AN IMPORTANT OMISSION: USING SCHOOL RESOURCES

Throughout our development of the previous editions of the **hm Program: Level I** we considered the inclusion of units related to students' use of school resources. Two key resources in our view were (1) the school library or media center, and (2) the guidance and special services personnel. Eventually we decided not to include units of this sort, because we could not direct them specifically enough to the situation in your school.

We have reached the same decision for this third edition for essentially the same reasons. Again we urge you to examine carefully your students' needs for skills in gaining access to and using school resources and to provide your students with the necessary instruction for developing them, if they are not receiving such instruction in another context.

INTRODUCTION TO STUDY SKILLS

The *Introduction to Study Skills* (pages 1-4 in the **Student Text)** involves your students in becoming more aware of how they learn. It also introduces them to the nature and value of study skills.

INTRODUCTION TO LEARNING AND STUDY SKILLS

HOW DO YOU LEARN?

Not everyone learns in the same way. There are many different ways to learn. Some people like to read about something new before they try it. Other people like to learn when they can actually "do" whatever they are learning. Some want to be able to imagine how to do something before they try it. Still others like to be told about a new thing. They like to discuss it before they try to do it. Can you think of any other ways that people learn to do new things?

The way you learn best is called your *learning style.*

EXERCISE I

Directions: What do you do well? Look at the list below, and pick *one* thing that you feel you have learned to do well. Or if you prefer, pick your own activity. Write your choice on the line below.

read	cook	debate
write	play a sport	use a word processor
sail	ride a bike	play a computer game
ski	find Internet information	knit
play an instrument	draw	care for an animal
sew	ice skate	solve math problems

_____

Do you remember when you were learning how to do the thing you chose? If not, cross it out and pick something you remember learning.

1

SUGGESTED DIRECTIONS FOR
INTRODUCTION TO LEARNING AND STUDY SKILLS

1. Pass out the **Student Text**. Have the students open to page 1. Read aloud *How Do You Learn?* Discuss briefly. You may want to focus on some of the discussion on the concept of learning style.

   Approximate time: 5 minutes

2. Read aloud the directions to Exercise I (page 1). Have the students follow these directions.

   3-5 minutes

EXERCISE II

Directions: Think about the thing you learned to do very well. How did you learn to do it?

Look at the words and phrases listed below. Circle the ones that describe how you learn best. You may also write other words and phrases that describe how you learn on the lines below.

Remember: There are no right or wrong answers! You can circle and write as many words and phrases as you need to describe how you learn.

watching	listening	doing
reading	thinking about	working when I have to
experimenting	writing	getting it right
learning from my mistakes	proving my point	"hands on"
being creative	talking it over with a friend	with a group
by myself	doing something I care about	asking questions
looking things up	practice	get a feeling that it's right

_____

_____

_____

_____

2

3. Read alout the directions to Exercise II (page 2). Have the students look over the list. Answer any questions they may have about the phrases. Then have your students do the exercise. When they have completed it, ask the students to share their responses to Exercises I and II. Then discuss as feels appropriate.

10 minutes

14

EXERCISE III

Directions: Look again at the list in EXERCISE I. This time pick out something that you've had *trouble* trying to learn well. Or if you prefer, pick your own activity. Write your choice on the line below.

_____

1. How did you try to learn the thing you said you had *trouble* learning? Look at the list in EXERCISE II again. Pick some ways that you tried to learn, and write these ways on the lines below.

   _____

   _____

   _____

2. Have you chosen any different ways than you chose for EXERCISE II? _____
   If you answered "yes," write the different ways on the lines below.

   _____

   _____

   _____

3

4. Read aloud the directions to Exercise III (page 3). Have the students complete the exercise. When they have done so, invite them to share their responses. Then discuss as feels appropriate.

   8 minutes

WHAT ARE LEARNING AND STUDY SKILLS?

Learning and study skills are **ways or methods for learning**. They are ways of doing what you are asked to do in school that can help you to learn better. When you use learning and study skills, you can often get more done in a given period of time and learn more, too.

Some examples of learning and study skills are these: active listening, tuning into directions, reading for meaning, taking notes, solving problems, and preparing for tests.

HOW DO YOU LEARN STUDY AND LEARNING SKILLS?

People learn study and learning skills through practice. You don't learn how to play basketball by talking about the game. You have to play it. The same is true with learning and study skills.

You often learn study and learning skills best through the mistakes you make. Everyone makes mistakes. What's important is that you look at your mistakes carefully and find out what caused them. When you know what caused a particular mistake, you'll know how not to make that mistake again.

WHY ARE LEARNING AND STUDY SKILLS IMPORTANT?

Learning won't suddenly become simple just because you have learned to use learning and study skills. But these skills will help you to become a better learner. You'll probably find school more rewarding and enjoyable. You'll also be more able to learn whatever you want outside of school.

4

5. Finish reading the *Introduction* (page 4) aloud with your students. Discuss.

   10 minutes

6. Orient your students to the *hm* **Study Skills Program** by presenting the following: a quick overview of the units in the **Program**, the value you see in learning and using these study skills, how you will use the **Program** in this class, and an evaluation of how the students work with the **Program**.

UNIT I: WAYS TO LISTEN

Listening skills are often overlooked during the middle school years, yet these skills are crucial to the achievement of academic success.

This unit provides your students with a learning experience about the effectiveness of their own listening skills. It also gives them a procedure in *Steps In Active Listening* that they can use to improve their listening skills.

In addition the unit provides you with an instrument with which you can gain a sense of (1) how well your students listen to you and (2) how well your students listen to each other. It also offers you a way to include the *Steps In Active Listening* in other areas of the curriculum.

A NOTE ABOUT TEACHING METHODS

In this unit, as with others in the **Program,** we have recommended that you organize your students into small work groups for the following reasons:

A. Working in small groups on a common task allows the students to learn skills through their interactions with each other.

B. Small group processes offer an effective method of engaging students in an activity. Such processes provide active participation for each and every student. Thus, small group processes both enhance motivation for learning and increase interest in the content of a lesson.

C. Small group instruction frees the teacher to become an observer in a more intimate way and to ascertain more accurately the level of instruction that will most benefit the students.

For those teachers who are not familiar with small group processes, we offer the following practical suggestions:

1. If you haven't done much small group work with your class, you may want to assign the initial groups. In each of the groups, try to create a healthy balance between students with good social skills and students with good task skills.

2. Make it clear to your students as to how and where the groups will be situated.

3. Move the whole class into groups at one time. This will help to minimize confusion.

4. Groups tend to work more effectively if they are functioning within time limits. Let your students know how much time they have to complete a given task.

5. When you first attempt group work, observe all of the groups and give them feedback on how well they are working as a group. Be sure that no group is dominated by any single individual. Pay as much attention to the process, at first, as you do to the product.

6. If you haven't done much group work, structure the first small group lessons with clear and specific task goals. Or break large tasks into small segments. After the groups have completed their work, allow time to examine how well each group worked toward the accomplishment of its goals.

7. Experiment with small group work! Eventually you'll find the balance that your class needs for effective small group processes.

Of course, individual work is of critical importance to the learning of skills. When a skill is introduced in a group setting, it becomes crucial to provide for individual work with that skill through homework and/or other class activities.

If you would like to examine the small group learning process in greater detail, we suggest that you look at one or more of the following resources:

Learning Together and Alone: Cooperation, Competition and Individualization by David W. Johnson and Roger T. Johnson (Allyn & Bacon, 1998)

The New Circles of Learning: Cooperation in the Classroom and School by David Johnson, Roger Johnson, and Edythe Johnson Holybec (ASCD, 1994)

Cooperative Learning: Resources for Teachers by Spencer Kagan (Resources for Teachers, 1990)

Cooperative Teaching: Rebuilding the Schoolhouse for All Students by Jeanne Bauwens and Jack Hourcade (PRO-ED Inc., 1995)

SUGGESTED DIRECTIONS FOR UNIT I

PLEASE NOTE: This unit requires two 40 minute class periods.

DAY 1

1. Remind your students about the values of the **hm Study Skills Program**. Remind them to pay attention to how they learn best.

Approximate time: 2 minutes

2. Two different ways of organizing the central activity of this unit, *The Listening Game,* are offered. Read through both sets of directions carefully, and select the method that you find more appropriate for your class.

First Alternative

1. Before class, make one copy of each *situation* (see pages 30-32 in the **Teacher's Guide**) on a separate piece of paper. At this time it would be helpful to examine all the *situations*.

2. At the beginning of the period, divide the class into small groups of 4-6 students. Have the members of each group sit together.

UNIT I: WAYS TO LISTEN

LISTENING IS MORE THAN JUST HEARING

The average student spends more than half of each school day *listening*. That means that you give more time to listening than to anything else you do in school.

Most people think of listening as something as natural as walking or eating. They don't think of it as anything you have to work at to do well. But we are not *born* good listeners. We learn to be good listeners.

Why is this so? Hearing is a natural ability, but *listening* is more than just hearing. Listening means directing your attention to — or *focusing on* — what you're hearing and trying to make sense of what you've heard.

Listening is a study skill. It's one of the most important study skills because listening is a part of almost everything else that you do. It seems simple, but it's not. Being a good listener doesn't come naturally. It requires learning and practice.

WHY IS IT HARD TO LISTEN EVEN WHEN YOU'RE INTERESTED?

Generally people talk at about 125 words per minute. However, we think at a speed that is more than three times as fast, about 400 words per minute. That means our thoughts move much faster than the words of whatever we're listening to. So it's not surprising that we often let our attention wander away from what another person is saying to us.

The key to becoming a good listener is to be an *active* listener: to keep your thoughts *focused* on what you are listening to.

5

3. Read aloud the passages on page 5 in the **Student Text.** Discuss briefly. Then read the directions to *The Listening Game* (page 6 in the **Student Text**) aloud to your class. Then select one student in each group to be a *reader.* Ask the members of the class who are not *readers* to answer the question in *When You Listen, What Do You Do?* (page 6 in the **Student Text**). While they are doing this, gather the *readers* together. Hand a different *situation* to each group *reader,* and explain to the readers that they will have to do the following tasks:

   a. Read your *situation* aloud to your group only *once.* Read slowly and clearly. Do not repeat anything. Also, do not answer any questions.

b. When you have finished reading, stay with your group. You may listen to the discussion, but do not participate in it.

c. When the groups have finished their work, switch groups with another *reader*. Now you become a *reporter*. Listen carefully to what the group members tell you about their *situation*. Remember as much as you can, but do not take notes. Be prepared to tell the entire class what the group has told you.

Ask the *readers* to read over their *situation* to themselves.

15 minutes

4. When your students have finished answering the question *When You Listen, What Do You Do?,* tell them that you will discuss their observations after they have played *The Listening Game.* Now explain to the group members that each group *reader* will read a story to them. Once the *reader* has finished reading, the members of the group must work to come to an agreement on what they've heard. Tell them they will have only seven minutes to reach an agreement.

Have the *readers* read the *situations* aloud. Then give the groups seven minutes to prepare. Have the *readers* switch groups and become the *reporters* after the seven minutes are over. Then have the groups tell the *reporters* what they have heard. Tell the *reporters* that they cannot ask any questions.

15-20 minutes

THE LISTENING GAME

Directions: A story will be read aloud to you only *once*. Pay close attention to the details of the story. When the story is finished, you will be asked to tell what you have heard. Listen carefully! (You are not allowed to take notes.)

WHEN YOU LISTEN, WHAT DO YOU DO?

The picture on the next page shows a classroom. It is almost the end of a class, and the teacher has given the students a few minutes to talk together. Read over their conversations.

Find the students who are called *Steve* and *Marybeth*.

Although Steve was not sitting with Marybeth's group, he heard what she had to say.

Why do you think he was able to give his attention to — or *focus on* — what Marybeth said? Write your answer on the lines below.

_____

_____

_____

_____

6

5. Ask one *reporter* to tell the class what his or her group has presented to him or her. Then read the original version of that situation aloud. Ask your students to suggest one or two ways in which the *situation* has been changed. List these on the board. Repeat the same process with the other *reporters* and *situations*. Then discuss the ways in which the situations have been changed through the listening process.

This is also a good time to discuss how your students learn: (1) by using the main ideas to remember details, or (2) by using details to remember main ideas. It may give you some insight into your students' learning styles.

15-20 minutes

PLEASE NOTE: You can also structure *The Listening Game* as a team contest. Just before the *reporters* share the information with the class, tell the teams that they can earn a point for each detail accurately reported. Then as you re-read the situation, have your students raise their hands when they hear a detail that has been reported by the reporter. Record a point for each detail mentioned by the *reporter*. This may help to encourage more active listening.

You will want to be careful not to make the contest so competitive that it becomes the main focus of attention.

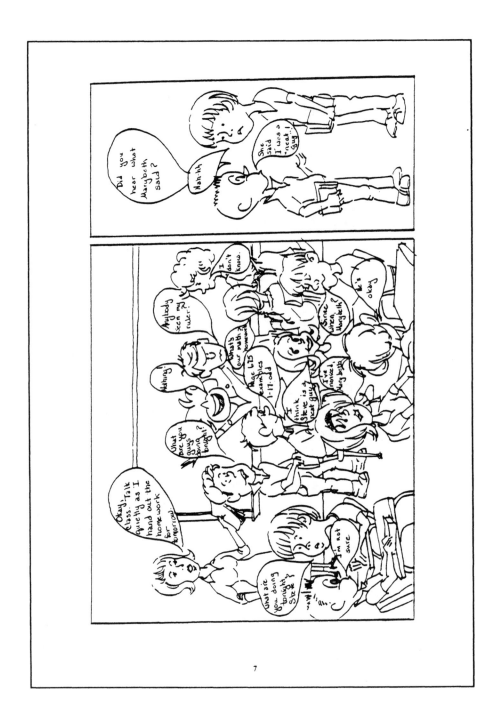

6. Go over the question *When You Listen, What Do You Do?* Discuss why it is easier to *focus* when you see the person you're listening to and you are interested in the topic.

    Also note to your students that when you *focus,* you block out other distractions. Ask the students to think about how they are able to do this and then to share their responses.

    Mention to the students that they can make the decision to be active listeners by *focusing* in the same way that they focus when they are intrigued enough to listen carefully.

    5-10 minutes

Second Alternative

1. Before class, make enough copies of *Situation B* for half your class; do the same with *Situation C*.

2. Read aloud the passages on page 5 in the **Student Text.** Then read the directions to *The Listening Game* (page 6 in the **Student Text**) aloud to your class. Then read *Situation A* aloud. Have two or three students give their version of what they have heard. Then read the original *situation* again, and discuss how the *situation* is changed through the listening process.

   Approximate time: 15 minutes

3. Divide the class into pairs. Pass out *Situation B* to one member of each pair, and *Situation C* to the other member. Have the students with *Situation B* read it aloud to their partners. Then have the listeners tell the readers what they have heard. Ask a student to read *Situation B* aloud to the class. Then discuss the students' experience of how the situation was changed through the listening process.

   10-15 minutes

4. Repeat the same process with *Situation C,* having the students reverse roles.

   10 minutes

5. Go over the question *When You Listen, What Do You Do?* (page 6 in the **Student Text**). Discuss why it is easier to *focus* when you see the person you're listening to and you are interested in the topic.

   Note that when you *focus,* you block out other distractions. Ask the students to think about how they are able to do this and share their responses.

   Explain to the students that they can make the decision to be active listeners by *focusing* in the same way that they focus when they are intrigued enough to listen carefully.

   8-10 minutes

DAY 2

In today's session, you will use the same teaching format that you used for *The Listening Game*. We strongly suggest that you prepare your own context paragraphs for this activity. Your students will benefit the most if the paragraphs relate directly to something you are currently teaching or wish to introduce. Workbooks, textbooks, and references can provide resources for appropriate paragraphs.

You will want to make sure that the paragraphs have a clearly stated main idea and several related details. It is also important for the content of the paragraphs to be about a topic that your students can visualize.

We have provided paragraphs with social studies content (**Teacher's Guide,** pages 33-35) if you choose not to select your own paragraphs. Please note that if you chose to do the *Second Alternative* with your students during *DAY 1,* you will have paragraphs D-F to use in today's session.

STEPS IN ACTIVE LISTENING

It is a *fact* that we can all become active listeners. So remember the word *FACT*. It will help you remember the steps in *active listening*, because the first letter of each of the steps spells the word *FACT*.

STEP # 1: FOCUS

The first step in active listening is to *focus*. This means to give your attention to something. Television often "catches" your attention. It doesn't require you to do the active work of *focusing*. However, when your father calls you from the next room as you are watching television, you have to pull your mind from the television to really **focus** on what he is saying.

STEP # 2: ASK

While you listen, *ask* yourself questions about what the speaker is saying. Then try to answer your questions, or see if the speaker answers them. Asking and answering questions in this way can help you make sense of the speaker's message.

When you are listening in school, you might *ask* yourself: what is it that the teacher wants me to know? Do I understand this? What don't I understand about what I am hearing? Does this make sense to me?

STEP # 3: CONNECT

Keep asking yourself why the speaker is saying what she or he is saying. Try to *connect* the main ideas with each other. For instance, the speaker may talk about growing food in a certain place. You already know that these things are needed for people to grow food: climate, soil conditions, and technology. As the speaker is talking, you will listen for and *connect* the main ideas of climate, soil conditions, and technology in order to understand how the food is grown.

STEP # 4: TRY TO PICTURE

Try to *picture in your mind* what the speaker is saying. Some people find that they can listen and remember better if they use their imaginations to make *mind pictures*. For example, if you are listening to a set of directions about how to get somewhere, make an imaginary map of the directions in your mind.

8

1. Read over the *Steps In Active Listening* with your students (page 8). Discuss each step, and relate it to *The Listening Game* that your students played the previous day.

    Approximate time: 10-15 minutes

TRY IT AGAIN - THE LISTENING GAME

Directions: Again a story will be read to you only *once*. Try out the *Steps To Active Listening*. *Focus* on the speaker so you can pay close attention to the details of the story. *Ask* yourself how these details *connect*. Try to *picture* what is happening.

When the story is finished, you will be asked to tell what you have heard.

1. Did you find listening any easier this time? _____

   If so, why? _____

   _____

2. Which of the *Steps* is the most difficult for you to do?

   _____

   Why do you think this is so? _____

   _____

   _____

UNIT I SUMMARY: WAYS TO LISTEN

We are not born as good listeners. We have to learn to listen well. Active listening is a study skill.

We can learn to listen actively by following these steps:

Focus
   Look at the speaker. Try to pay attention to what is being said.

Ask questions
   Try to figure out what is important by asking questions. Then answer your questions, or see if the speaker answers your questions.

Connect
   "Make sense" out of what the speaker is saying by *connecting* main ideas with each other.

Try to picture
   Try to see "in your mind's eye" what the speaker is talking about.

9

2. Repeat the procedure you used for *The Listening Game* during *DAY 1* with *Try It Again — The Listening Game* (page 9). Use your own paragraphs or the ones prepared for you in the **Teacher's Guide.**

   15-20 minutes

3. Have the students answer questions # 1 and # 2 (page 9) when they finish *Try It Again — The Listening Game.*

    When they have done so, discuss your students' answers to the questions.

    Read over the *Summary.* Highlight the steps in active listening. Explain to your students how they can use the acronym "FACT" to help them remember the four steps.

    10 minutes

SITUATION A

We are all witnesses to an automobile accident. Listen carefully as I read to you what we have all "seen."

We were all standing at the intersection of South Street and East Avenue in Turner's Falls, Missouri. It was late in the morning. A blue sedan, carrying only a driver, slowed, signaled, and made a right turn from South Street onto East Avenue without bothering to obey the stop sign.

The truck racing up East Avenue caught the side of the sedan's rear bumper. The sedan spun into a fire hydrant, breaking the hydrant in two. A flow of water came rushing out from the hydrant stump, and the neighborhood children were soon splashing in the water on this hot July day.

SITUATION B

We are all witnesses to a bank robbery. Listen carefully as I read to you what we all have "seen."

At 1:00 PM we were standing in the lobby of the Bank of Canada in Edmonton, Alberta. Three persons dressed in clown outfits with faces painted white skipped into the bank. Each wore the same costume, except that one had a red hat, another a green one, and the third, a yellow one.

The clown with the red hat went to the teller at the last window while the other two clowns juggled oranges in the middle of the bank. Then the clown with the yellow hat began to shout advertisements for the circus. The clown with the green hat went from person to person selling tickets until the bank manager came out to chase the two of them away. By the time he got both clowns out through the revolving doors, the clown in the red hat had also disappeared.

A minute later the bank manager walked to the last window. He found that the teller had fainted and that $5,000 was missing from the drawer.

SITUATION C

We are all witnesses to a rescue on the beach. Listen carefully as I read to you what we have all "seen."

We were all standing on the edge of the beach on Pelican Lake, which is located just outside Silver Springs, Georgia. It was just after noon because we had heard the noon bell from the fire station only a few minutes before.

A boy of about ten years was fishing from a rowboat. His line jerked fiercely, and he stood up to reel in what might be a big catch. As he started to pull it in, a motorboat towing a water skier roared by. The skier's wake rolled up against the rowboat and knocked the boy into the water.

A big Labrador Retriever swam out into the lake and grabbed the boy by the collar of his shirt. Both boy and dog made it safely back to shore, and the motorboat vanished around the bend in the lake.

SITUATION D

We are all witnesses to a tornado. Listen carefully as I read to you what we all have "seen."

It was August 29th, a very hot and humid day in Wellcove, Texas. We were sitting on the front porch of our house trying to cool off. It was already late in the afternoon when we noticed the sky turning a bright yellow. A few minutes later we saw funnel-shaped clouds coming in from the west.

We knew that they were tornado clouds, so we ran into the basement for safety. Through the basement window, we saw a pick-up truck lifted up by the wind and set down on the top of Newberry's Department Store. On the other side of our street, all the windows were broken.

Later we found out that some of the stores such as the hardware store also had their insides knocked out. But others weren't damaged much at all. In the ice cream parlor, the cones were stacked in neat piles on the counter just behind the broken windows. On our side of the street, nothing was touched at all, except for a barber pole that was knocked over.

31

SITUATION E

We are all witnesses to a poodle kidnapping. Listen carefully as I read to you what we have all "seen."

It was April 15th, a warm day in San Francisco. We were all waiting in the TWA boarding lounge at the airport. Our jet was scheduled to leave for New york in fifteen minutes.

A gray miniature poodle with pink bows tied on its head was sitting on the lap of a well-dressed woman. Many people had stopped to pat the little dog on the head and ask the woman how it was going to travel aboard the airplane. She was explaining the airline rules and the dog's black carrying case to an elderly man when a firecracker exploded about two feet away. The dog bolted into the crowd.

We saw a man in a gray raincoat pick up the dog and run through the crowd into a room marked "Employees Only." We watched until we had to board the plane. Nobody entered or left the room.

SITUATION F

We are all witnesses to a window cleaner's accident. Listen carefully as I read to you what we all have "seen."

It was early in the morning of September 11, a bright and warm day. We had just arrived at work on the top floor of the old Crest Building in Baltimore. A few minutes later, we saw the window cleaner appear on the scene. He spent almost an hour setting up pulleys and a platform. Then he was finally ready to step out onto the platform and clean the windows.

About an hour later we saw a huge orange balloon floating past the windows. The balloon was about 60 feet tall. Hanging from the bottom of the balloon was a wicker basket with a young woman standing in it. The basket swung too close to the building and appeared to knock the window cleaner off the platform. We all rushed to the window to see what had happened. The woman in the basket had grabbed the window cleaner. His feet were kicking in mid air. Finally they glided away from the building and landed safely in a chestnut tree in the middle of the park across the street.

PILGRIM 1

I am going to read a paragraph about the Pilgrims' preparations for leaving England. Listen carefully, and try to picture what I am saying.

During the summer of 1606 the Pilgrims planned how to get out of England. They wanted to go to another country where they would be free to worship as they chose. It was not easy. King James did not like his subjects to find homes in other lands. When autumn came, crops were gathered and sold. The men secretly got rid of their horses and cattle, their furniture, and most of their other belongings. Clothing, bedding, and a few of their smaller treasures were packed into bundles that they could carry. At last they were ready to start, though they had no permission to make the journey. They knew they had to leave England to avoid arrest, but they were sad at the thought of going. They loved their homeland. They loved the green fields and the meadows around Scrooby and the home in which they had once been happy.

PILGRIM 2

I am going to read a paragraph about the Pilgrims' second attempt to reach Holland. Listen carefully, and try to picture what I am saying.

On their second attempt to reach Holland — the country the Pilgrims had chosen to live in so they could practice their religion — the men and boys were successful. The women and young children were arrested but eventually were allowed to join the men. Here's what happened. Wiliam Brewster arranged with a Dutch captain to have a Dutch ship carry the Pilgrims to Holland. Careful plans were made to meet at a lonely spot on the shore between the cities of Grimsby and Hull. The women and children, with most of their possessions, traveled to the meeting place in a small boat they had hired. The men and boys planned to go overland to the spot. The women and children arrived a day early, and the seas were rough. They begged the sailors to pull into a muddy creek near the spot where they were to meet the Dutch captain. On the meeting day, the tiny boat was stranded when the tide went out. They were unable to sail to their men who had met up as planned with the Dutch captain. The Dutch captain, meanwhile, was in no mood to wait. He had seen the long black line of the King's horsemen curving down the hillside heading straight for the meeting spot. Although the men and boys made it on board, the still stranded women and children were arrested. The King eventually allowed them to join their menfolk in Holland.

PILGRIM 3

I am going to read a paragraph about the Pilgrims' settlement in Leyden, Holland. Listen carefully, and try to picture what I am saying.

When the Pilgrims first left England so they could practice their religion as they pleased, they settled in Amsterdam, Holland. They found that making a living in Amsterdam was difficult. Soon they were on the move again to Leyden, Holland. Leyden was a beautiful city with a great university, fields of beautiful flowers, and meadows of white linen that had been stretched out to bleach in the sun. But Leyden proved to be even a harder place than Amsterdam to make a living. William Brewster, who had a good education, taught English and printed books. But most of the men had been simple farmers in England. They found that they had to go to work in the cloth mills. Some got jobs washing wool, as it was very dirty when clipped from the sheep. Others combed it. Still others spun it into thread, while many of the men wove the thread into cloth. Work started as soon as it was light and continued until dark. And still the families earned so little money that even the boys and girls had to go to work in the mills. The Pilgrims began to think about leaving Holland.

PILGRIM 4

I am going to read a paragraph about the Pilgrims' opportunity to go to the New World. Listen carefully, and try to picture what I am saying.

Although living in Holland allowed the Pilgrims to practice their religious beliefs, they found that making a living was difficult. They also missed the English language and English customs. They began to dream of sailing to the New World where they could truly be themselves. But it was an expensive proposition to sail halfway around the globe, and the Pilgrims were poor. Finally a man named Thomas Weston said he and a group of businessmen would put up the needed money. He set hard terms. He agreed that his company would advance much of the money needed if the settlers, in turn, would promise to work for him for seven years fishing, lumbering, farming, and fur trading, or anything else they could find to do. Nothing the settlers earned or made for seven long years would be their own. Even the clothes on their backs and the houses they built with their own hands would belong to the company. This was almost the same as slavery and the Pilgrims knew it, but they had no other choice. Soon many of them had signed up to sail to the New World under Weston's terms.

PILGRIM 5

I am going to read a paragraph about the Pilgrims' voyage on the Mayflower. Listen carefully, and try to picture what I am saying.

The Mayflower was designed to be a freighter, not a passenger ship. But it was to carry 102 passengers, including the future colony of Pilgrims, across the Atlantic to the New World. People were crowded everywhere on this tiny freighter. There were only a few passenger bunks and one cabin. Most of the women with small children were jammed into this cabin. All the rest "camped out" as best they could. Some slept between decks, and some of the boys and younger men curled up in the bottom of a shallop, a fishing boat that had been stowed on the gun deck. The Mayflower was well armed. She carried large guns called "minions," which would shoot cannon balls at any attacking pirate ship. She also had smaller guns called "sakers" as well as a supply of muskets and cutlasses to use for hand-to-hand combat. There was no heat on the Mayflower, no toilet except a bucket that had to be emptied overboard, no bathroom, no way to get cleaned up. Like their parents, the children wore the same clothes day after day, week after week, getting dirtier all the time. This tiny ship designed for trade provided uncomfortable quarters for the three month journey across the ocean.

These paragraphs were adapted from Margaret Pumphrey's *Pilgrim Stories* (New York: Rand McNally, 1961).

ADDITIONAL SUGGESTIONS

1. Create enjoyable activities that encourage your students to listen well. If they feel successful about listening in "game" type activities, they will also feel positive about listening in other learning activities. Some ways you can do this are the following:

    A. Get road map sets for your class. Put your students in pairs. Have the partners each decide on a destination. Each student should mark his or her own route in red. Taking turns, the partners give directions to each other on how to follow their created routes. The listeners mark the new route in blue. Afterwards they compare routes to see how well they listened.

    B. The *Listening Game* format is a good way to introduce a new unit in science or social studies. Find paragraphs that outline a main idea of the unit and contain several details. Read the paragraphs aloud. Ask the students to restate the main idea and repeat as many details as they can remember.

    C. There are many cooperative games that require students to listen to each other as well as to the instructor. A good resource for these types of learning activities is *Everyone Wins: Cooperative Games and Activities* by Sambhava and Josette Luvmour (New Society Publishers, 1996).

    D. Use the same kind of motivation taught by games in your classroom teaching. For example, when doing a science experiment, say, "We're going to prove air takes up space. Maybe you could show your parents the same experiment tonight and explain to them what you have learned."

2. Effective listening skills are often closely related to the child's ability to visualize what he or she is hearing. You can help your students learn to visualize more effectively by providing them with practice in listening *and* visualizing. For example, read a description of the eye or the heart and ask the students to draw or diagram what they have heard. (Assure your students that they need not have any skill in drawing.) Or use descriptions of a battle, an imaginary creature, or a kind of food. Or you can lead your students through an imaginery experience of some physical activity before they conduct the activity physically. Be sure to integrate this kind of exercise into the regular curriculum of your class. Also, be careful to ask your students to draw or diagram something that is relatively simple but that requires attention to detail. You can use *SITUATION A* from this unit as an example of how visualizing helps you to remember. Review that situation, and draw it on the board or use the overhead projector. Then design a similar situation to read to your class. Have them map it out as you read it.

3. There are three general kinds of listening:

  a) Listening for information and organization;

  b) Critical listening;

  c) Listening for appreciation and enjoyment.

  Involve your students in experiences that are directed to each of these kinds of listening. Explain to your students that there are different ways to listen. For instance, when you read a story to them, you will want them to imagine the setting and characters to help them remember the main parts of the story. This is different from trying to remember the sequence to a set of directions. It helps to tell them what type of a listening task they have to do, what they must listen for, and what they will do as a result of listening.

4. Teach your students to listen carefully to you! Try not to repeat instructions. Instead, from the very first day of the school year, accustom your class to the expectation that you will say things only *once*. (You may find this a struggle in the beginning, but the rewards for everyone are worth the effort.)

  Explain to your students that you will allow clarifying questions. Invite them to ask these kinds of questions at the end of a set of directions.

  If you are giving a complicated set of directions, explain to the students that you will repeat yourself and also explain why you are repeating yourself.

5. Give your students the opportunity to use the *Steps In Active Listening* on page 8. Create learning experiences that illustrate each step.

6. There are several commercially prepared listening programs such as *Basic Skill Series — Listening Skills* by Janie Schmidt (Instructional Fair, Inc., 1998) and *Listening and Following Directions #3 and #4* (Steck Vaughn, 1994). These programs present a main idea and require students to listen to an instructor for details. It is best to preview the programs so you can find exercises that fit into the style and the content of your class.

7. Involve any other teachers that work with your students in your strategies for active listening. You might want to share the *Steps In Active Listening* with your colleagues. For example, a physical education teacher in a school that had adopted the *Steps* might hold up a red flag every time she or he wanted the students to *focus*. This provides a good reinforcement for a term that the students use in their academic classes.

UNIT II: TUNING INTO DIRECTIONS

By this age, students are well acquainted with many of the standard practices that we use in the classroom. As a result of this familiarity as well as other factors, they often do not read or listen to directions carefully. Instead they make assumptions about directions based on their previous experience. Even your best students may try to outguess you and begin an assignment before you have even completed the instructions.

This unit can help students begin to recognize the importance of attending carefully to both oral and written directions. There are two exercises in this unit. The first one focuses the students' awareness on the task of listening to and following directions. The second exercise gives your students an opportunity to sharpen the skills they must use when listening to and following directions. You may want to design a different second exercise that more closely fits your own curriculum.

In Exercise I the first direction that you give tells your students that they will spell a word in crayon. As the students look at the diagram on page 10 of the **Student Text**, many of your students will immediately perceive the word "listen." Some may go to work at once as a result of this perception, without listening to you and following the other instructions. As the task progresses, you may lose others.

The purpose of this exercise is not to trick your students but to help both you and them discover at what point they tune you out and no longer attend to your instructions. This activity provides you with a diagnostic tool in reference to your students' skill in reading and listening to directions and following them. You may also wish to ask those students who get the "wrong answer" to examine their own experience of this game. Ask them to see if they can discover when and why they "tuned out" your directions.

The second exercise provides a means through which your students can practice whatever went "wrong" in the first exercise. It also gives students an opportunity to experience the difficulty involved in giving clear directions.

PLEASE NOTE: Prior to teaching this unit, you'll need to make a transparency copy of the map on page 13 for use with an overhead projector. You'll need that copy, an overhead projector, and a screen for Exercise II in this unit.

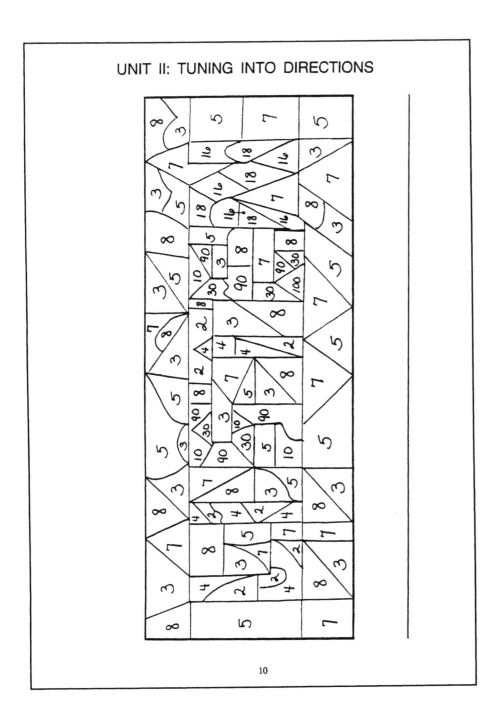

UNIT II: TUNING INTO DIRECTIONS

10

SUGGESTED DIRECTIONS FOR UNIT II

1. Read all of Exercise I carefully. The "trick" to this activity is presented on page 11 of the **Student Text.** The last two paragraphs instruct students to follow only directions #3, #7, and #9. If they play the game correctly, they will create the word *lit.* If they play it incorrectly, the word will be *listen.*

2. Make sure that each student has a pencil and a crayon.

3. Tell your students that they will be playing a game that will show how well they listen to and follow directions.

Read the directions below aloud. (These directions begin with "Open your **Study Skills Programs**..." and conclude with direction # 10.) Read slowly and clearly. Be sure to read each number as well as each direction. Pause for about five seconds between directions. The last direction is the most important one, but don't overemphasize it.

DIRECTIONS

Open your **Study Skills Programs** to page 10. This unit is called *Tuning Into Directions,* and we're going to play a game involving following directions. Now turn your books so that the numbers on the diagram are right side up. (Pause to make sure this is done.)

I'm going to read a set of directions to you. *Don't do anything* until I have finished reading the whole set of directions. Then I will read them again, but only one more time. Use the first reading as a preview. You will need this reading to keep in tune for the second reading.

1. One clue is that you will end up with a word spelled out in crayon when you are done with this game. Another clue is that there is a trick to the game.

2. Color in pencil all spaces containing the number seven.

3. Color in crayon all spaces containing the number two.

4. Color in crayon all spaces containing multiples of ten. (If your students are not familiar with this concept, you can say all numbers that end in zero instead.)

5. Color in pencil all spaces containing the number eight.

6. Color in crayon all spaces containing even numbers between eleven and nineteen.

7. Color in crayon all spaces containing the number four.

8. Color in pencil all spaces containing the number five and the number three.

9. Write the word that you have spelled out on the line below the diagram. If you have the correct word, you have won the game!

10. You will not need this direction the second time through, but now it is important. You will find information that you need to win this game on page 11. Turn to page 11 now, and read it carefully. You will have _____* minutes to do this.

   *Decide how much time your students will need to read page 11, and tell them that they will have that amount of time when you read direction # 10.

Approximate time: 20 minutes

40

EXERCISE I

TUNING INTO DIRECTIONS

You will find that listening to and following directions is a very important skill. This is true not only in schoolwork but also in your daily life. Probably each of you has a story about a time when you only half heard or didn't hear a direction. Afterwards you found yourself in a complete mess, like the man in the old joke:

He thought they said "trains" when they passed out brains, so he ran to catch one. Never got himself a brain!

It seems that the man in the joke shares a problem with many people. Recently the students in a midwestern school received very poor grades on an achievement test. When they investigated the cause of these results, guidance counselors and classroom teachers found not poor students but poor listeners. These students had never taken this kind of test before. They weren't tuned in to listening to and following directions. So they could only guess at what they were supposed to do.

You can't guess about directions and expect to be right! You need to listen carefully and ask questions if you don't understand what you have heard.

You are already showing that you are a good listener because you are reading this page as you were instructed. Now here's an important clue! You must listen to and follow only directions #3, #7, and #9 the next time your teacher reads the directions.

The students in the midwestern school were then taught how to listen to directions. They also learned to read directions more carefully. When they took the achievement test again, they did much better. After you have read this page carefully, keep the secret to yourself! Write 3, 7, and 9 on the page before this one so you will know what directions to follow. Listen carefully, follow the right directions, and you will spell the right word in crayon.

11

4. When the students have completed their reading, repeat directions #1 - #9. Pause about 20-30 seconds after each direction.

7-9 minutes

5. Tell your students that the winning word is *lit*. Discuss the importance of following the directions in this game. Engage your students in trying to figure out where they "went wrong" by asking questions such as the following ones:

When did you think you knew the answer? Why did seeing the word "listen" in the diagram make it difficult for you to follow directions?

Did you start following the directions on the first reading? Why did you do that? How many felt that the directions were so long and confusing that you had to start right away?

Did you read carefully?

Did anyone follow the directions accurately but not believe the word could be something other than "listen"?

Can you think of any other time when you jumped ahead because you thought you knew what you were doing and got into trouble as a result?

5-10 minutes

6. Announce that your class will take an imaginary "field trip" to Washington, D.C. Project the map on your screen. Then describe the "field trip" by saying something like the following:

"You will be touring the area around the Washington Mall during one day of this field trip. The Washington Mall area contains many government buildings and also many national monuments and museums. You get to plan this part of the trip yourself. However, a partner must know where you are at all times. So, you need to do three things:

1. plan your own trip;
2. give directions to your partner about your plan; and
3. take directions from your partner about his or her plan.

"Please turn to page 13. There are many places of interest on the Washington Mall. You will only have time to stop at five places of interest, including your beginning and ending places."

Then read aloud the first place on the list below. Locate it on the overhead map, and direct your students to find it on their own maps. Follow the same procedure with each place on the list.

Lincoln Memorial
National Academy of Science
Federal Reserve Building
Bureau of Indian Affairs
The White House
The Executive Offices
Treasury Department
General Sherman Statue
National Museum of Natural History

National Art Gallery
General Meade Statue
General Grant Statue
The Capitol
Botanic Gardens
Smithsonian Institution
Air and Space Museum
Washington Monument

8-10 minutes

7. Go on by saying something like the following:

"Find the heading at the top of page 12 called *Possible Beginnings and Ends*. These places are choices of where to start and end your journey. For example, you might *start* here (show the students on an overhead projector) at the Lincoln Memorial and *end* here (again show the students on the map) at the Capitol.

"Now choose your beginning and end. Don't mark anything on the map yet. Just decide in your mind. You will have one minute to do this."

3 minutes

8. Have your students read over the *Directions for Making Your Map* on page 12. Give them time to do so.

   Then have them follow these directions. (You may need to explain what a mall or block is so that your students can follow direction #4.) Give your students time to follow the directions.

   10-15 minutes

9. Go on to say something like the following:

   "You are now ready for *Giving Directions-Procedure* (page 14). You must tell your partner exactly where you will be. You will use the second map on page 15 to mark in your partner's route."

   Have your students read *Giving Directions-Procedure* on page 14. Give your students three to five minutes to do so. When they have read *Giving Directions-Procedure,* invite questions and respond to them. When you get to #4, ask the students if they have any other suggestions for how to give clear directions. Invite questions and respond to them. Then read aloud **Rules and Pointers** (page 14), and discuss briefly.

   10-12 minutes

10. Have the students organize themselves into pairs. Ask each pair to decide who will give directions first. Explain that once a pair has gone through all of the steps in *Giving Directions-Procedure,* they should switch roles and work through the steps again.

    Ask the students to begin the activity. Circulate among them as they work. Make sure that the students do not show each other their maps but rely on listening skills. Also, make sure that the listeners do not speak.

    Take note of the students' techniques for giving directions. Look for such things as the following:

    Clarity of directional terms such as "beside," "on top of," "to the left of," "around the corner," "up the street."

    Speakers who are aware of the time it takes for someone to locate places and follow directions and thus speak slowly and clearly.

    Speakers who prepare the listeners for following directions by saying such things as the following: "Find Pennsylvania Avenue. It runs northwest and southeast."

    15-20 minutes

44

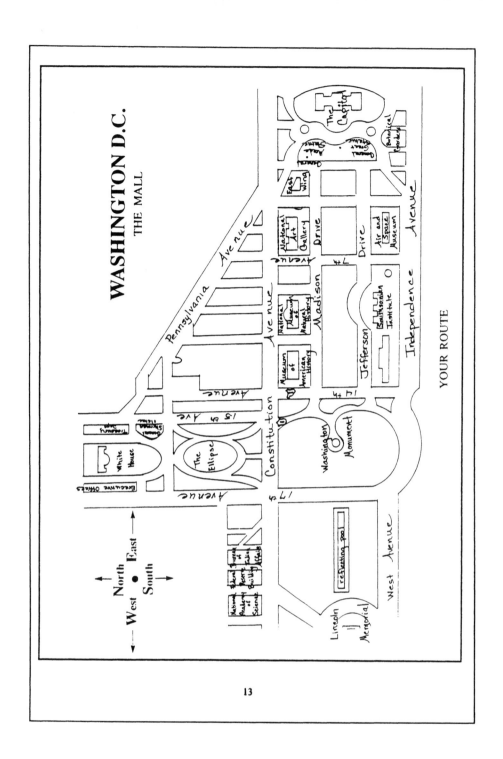

WASHINGTON D.C.

THE MALL

YOUR ROUTE

North
West — East — South

The Capitol

Botanical Gardens

General Grant Statue

Mall Street

East Wing

National Art Gallery

7th Avenue

Drive

Air and Space Museum

Independence Avenue

National Museum of Natural History

Madison Drive

Smithsonian Institute

Museum of American History

Jefferson Drive

4th

7th

Constitution Avenue

Avenue

15 Ave

Pennsylvania Avenue

The Ellipse

Washington Monument

Treasury Dept

General Sherman Statue

White House

Executive Offices

Avenue

17th

West Avenue

reflecting pool

National Academy of Science

Federal Reserve Building

Bureau of Indian Affairs

Lincoln Memorial

13

45

Giving Directions – Procedure

1. Tell your partner where to start. Have your partner mark that spot with a star.

2. Give directions to get to the first point of interest. Have your partner mark that spot with an arrow.

3. Give directions to get to your second point of interest. Have your partner mark that spot with an arrow.

4. Give directions to get to your third point of interest. Have your partner mark that spot with an arrow.

5. Give directions to get to your end spot. Have your partner mark that spot by circling it.

6. Compare maps. See how closely your routes match.

Rules and Pointers

1. All of your directions must be spoken. You may not show your map to your partner or point things out on your partner's map.

2. The listener is not allowed to say anything. This means that the listener may not ask questions or ask the speaker to repeat or wait.

3. When you are giving directions, speak slowly and clearly.

4. Use the names of roads, avenues, and streets. (Be aware that some streets are unnamed.)

14

11. When your students have completed the exercise, invite them to discuss their experience. As feels helpful, share with them your observations of their strengths and weaknesses in giving directions. Also ask the students to describe in what ways they used *Steps In Active Listening* in this activity.

    5-10 minutes

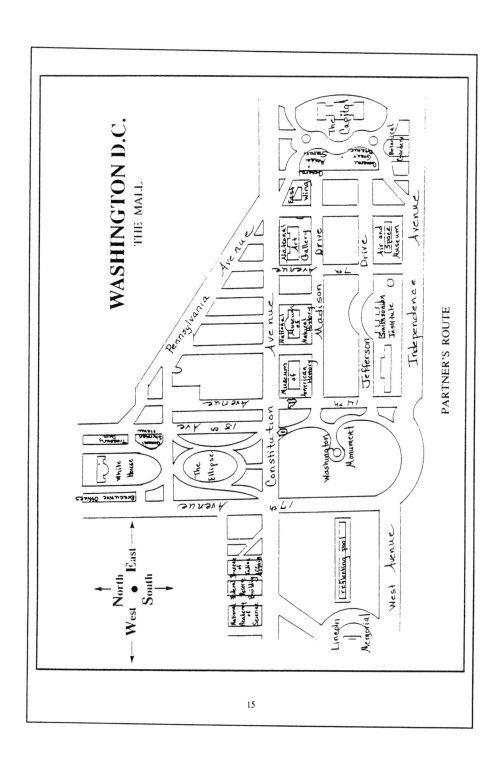

WASHINGTON D.C.
THE MALL

PARTNER'S ROUTE

UNIT II SUMMARY: TUNING INTO DIRECTIONS

Remember the STEPS IN ACTIVE LISTENING from Unit I. They are these:

Focus

Look at the speaker. Try to pay attention to what is being said.

Ask questions

Try to figure out what is important by asking questions. Then answer your questions, or see if the speaker answers your questions.

Connect

Make sense out of what the speaker is saying by *connecting* main ideas with each other.

Try to picture

Try to see *in your mind's eye* what the speaker is talking about.

Reading and listening to directions is an important skill. This is true not only in school but in any situation in life.

Read directions carefully. Be sure to read *all* of the directions. Then if you don't understand, ask questions. If you are not allowed to ask questions, ask yourself the questions and listen for the answers.

Listen carefully when someone is giving you directions. Don't try to guess what they are. Listen to *all* of the directions. Then if you don't understand what you've heard, ask questions.

If you can't remember all the directions, write them down on a piece of paper.

16

ADDITIONAL SUGGESTIONS

1. Divide your class into pairs. Let one student be the *director* and the other be the *follower*. Give each student a copy of a maze like the one below. (You may want to create a more difficult maze.) Ask the *directors* to draw a path through the maze. Tell them not to let their partners see their path. Then have the *directors* give oral directions to the *followers* about how to get through the maze. The object of the instructions is for the *follower* to draw a path through the maze exactly like that of the *director*. When the students have finished, ask them to compare the two paths. You "win" if the two paths are identical. Have the students switch roles and repeat the exercise.

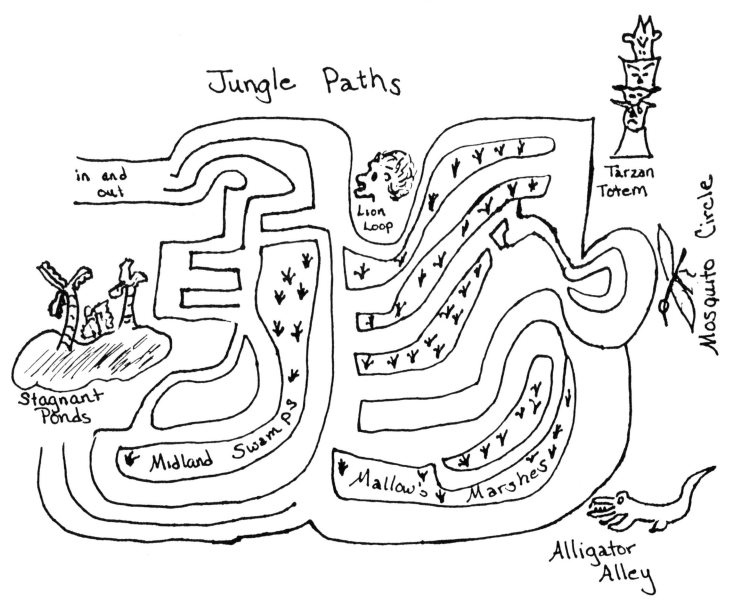

2. Involve your class in playing the game of *Airplane and Pilot*. In this game, one student is blind-folded. She or he is the *airplane*. The classroom is then set up into an obstacle course. Choose a *pilot* to land the *airplane* successfully by giving her or him oral directions. Repeat the game with a new *airplane, pilot,* and obstacle course.

3. There are many fine origami books. These books can provide excellent, concrete examples of how to follow written directions. Students working in pairs will also gain practice in working with oral directions as inevitably one student will be able to tell the other how to fit certain designs together. A book that may interest your students is *The Best Jumbo Paper Aircraft* by Campbell Morris (Putnam, 1993).

4. You can find a variety of exercises that require students to follow directions in *Following Directions Using Ancient Civilizations as a Theme* (Instructional Fair, Inc., 1996) and in *Who's Following Direction: A Learning Works Skill Builder* (Learning Works, 1999). If you want to integrate math and listening/following directions, you can find activities in *Listen Up Math* by Ann Fisher (Teaching and Learning Co., 1994).

5. Cut out identical sets of shapes from sheets of tagboard. You can also use commercial attribute sets. Have a set of shapes for each student.

    Organize your class into pairs, with one member of each pair identified as A and the other as B. Have the pairs sit backtoback on the floor. Give each student an identical set of shapes.

    Have the A's arrange their shapes into a figure design. When they have done so, have each A give directions to her or his partner so that the partner can make an exact copy of the A's design or figure without looking at it.

    This activity is especially rich because certain discrepancies in giving directions emerge. Students have to decide if "on top of" looks like this:

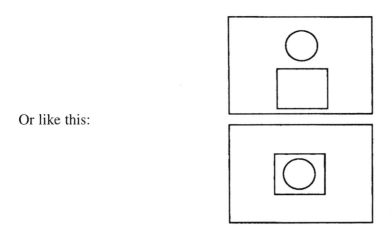

Or like this:

    After one attempt and discussion, have the A's and B's switch roles and try again.

    You can also have your students write out directions for the arrangement of the shapes and see if a partner can follow the written directions.

6. In the beginning of a new school year, it is always fun to play an *Introductions Game.* This is an activity that begins by putting your students in a circle.

Choose a student to begin by introducing himself or herself, telling the class one important thing about himself or herself, and leaving an opening for the person on his or her right to introduce himself or herself. For example:

"Hi, my name is Mark. I wonder how I'll like this new school. This is . . ."

The next person must introduce herself or himself as well as all the people who have gone before her or him.

"My name is Carey. Our family just got a new German shepherd. This is Mark, he is wondering if he'll like this school. This is . . . "

Work through the circle until all members of the class are introduced.

7. As part of a writing assignment, have your students go to a designated part of the school to "eavesdrop." Students are asked to write down *everything* that they hear, then incorporate these sounds (the bits of conversation, the scraping of chairs across a tiled floor, the clink of silverware as it hits the tray) into a descriptive piece about that place. You might start this activity by bringing in a tape recording of the cafeteria or any other busy place in your school and involving your class in listing just how many sounds can be heard.

8. Select a written passage from any subject area to read to your students. Change certain words or phrases throughout the passage so that their meaning becomes nonsensical or irrelevant. Ask your students to listen and think about the passage as you read it aloud at an even pace. Have your students raise their hands whenever they hear words that do not make sense. Review the passage orally or on an overhead projector to discuss the changed wording.

You can create humorous irregularities or insert incorrect ideas in subject matter that your students are currently studying. Start out with fairly obvious miscues. Then increase the level of subtlety as your students become more discriminating.

As a variation, have your students keep a count on paper during a first reading. Compare the number of "mistakes" that the students heard. Then have your students raise their hands as described above during a second reading of the passage.

UNIT III: GETTING THE TIMING DOWN

Sequencing is a thinking skill that helps students to organize information in relation to time. This skill, which we call "getting the timing down," is important for students to learn as they become aware of patterns within narratives and how such patterns relate to cause and effect.

The exercises in this unit introduce your students to the concept and the skill of sequencing. Your students will also use sequencing skill to predict outcomes based on a knowledge of prior events in a narrative.

In addition this unit involves your students in a review of the listening and direction-following skills introduced in the first two units.

Your students' experience with these exercises will provide you with insight into how your students organize and use their own sense of timing.

UNIT III: GETTING THE TIMING DOWN

INTRODUCTION

When you read or hear a story, you can understand it better if you know the order in which the events are taking place. Knowing the order of events means that you know what happened first, what happened next, and so on.

Another way of saying this is that you know the *sequence* of events. The *sequence* is the order in which the events take place.

"Getting the timing down" means to understand the sequence of events in a story. Sometimes people call "getting the timing down" by another name: *sequencing*.

The exercises in this unit will help you learn more about "getting the timing down" or *sequencing*.

17

SUGGESTED DIRECTIONS FOR UNIT III

PLEASE NOTE: This unit will require two 40 minute class periods.

DAY 1

1. Your students can complete the exercises in this unit individually, in pairs, or in small groups. Or you may want your students to do some of these exercises alone and others with a partner or partners. Look through the unit, and decide what approach will be the most helpful with your class.

2. Read the *Introduction* (page 17) aloud, or have a student or students read it aloud. Discuss briefly for clarity and emphasis.

    Approximate time: 5-8 minutes

3. Read aloud the directions to Exercise I, *Philip's Story* (page 18), to your students. Then have your students work on the exercise. (With a young class, you may want to read the paragraphs and instructions aloud also and discuss how to begin the exercise.)

When your students have completed the exercise, go over their answers. Discuss how your students developed their sequence of events. A "correct" sequence is given in the *Answers For Exercises In Unit III* (page 65). Your students may develop other sequences. In your discussion, be sure to talk about why one sequence can be more "correct" than others.

15-20 minutes

PHILIP'S NEIGHBORHOOD

19

55

KEY WORDS: TIME QUALIFIERS

When you read or listen to a story, you will often find key words that can give you an idea about *when* events in the story take place. These key words are *time qualifiers*. These words qualify other words or phrases. To qualify is to make the meaning of words or phrases clearer.

Some examples of *time qualifiers* that tell you more about when events take place are these:

while	during	before
after	as	until
following	afterwards	in the meantime

There are many other *time qualifiers*. Any word or phrase that helps you to understand when events are happening is a *time qualifier*.

4. Have your students read *Key Words: Time Qualifiers* (page 20), or read it aloud to them. Discuss briefly. Then go over the directions for Exercise II (page 21) orally. Do the two examples as a class. Then have your students complete the exercise. Go over the sentences, and discuss.

10-15 minutes

EXERCISE II

Directions: Each of the sentences below includes two events. In each sentence, circle the word(s) that you recognize as a *time qualifier*. Then underline the event that happens first.

If the events in a sentence are happening at the same time, do not underline anything.

EXAMPLES

Before Molly left for school, she ate two pieces of toast.

We set up the tents while the others gathered firewood.

1. I had a great time after I got to know all of the people there.

2. Before Miguel had realized the danger he was in, he was enjoying sailing over the wild waves.

3. Darcy searched for clues to the disappearance of her brother, Ted, but in the meantime, he slept soundly, unaware that she was trying to find him.

4. It had taken years of hard work, but finally the statue was finished.

5. Following the wedding ceremony, there was a reception at the Martin Luther King Community Center.

6. Water expands when it is cooled.

7. As the ice masses drew back, they carved lakes and hills upon the earth's surface.

8. Divide the money equally among yourselves, and then go to the store.

9. All during the time I had been outdoors planting, the baby had been playing happily in her pen.

10. The water pressure built up until the dam finally cracked.

21

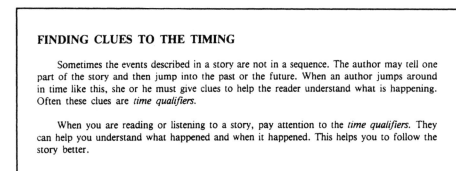

FINDING CLUES TO THE TIMING

Sometimes the events described in a story are not in a sequence. The author may tell one part of the story and then jump into the past or the future. When an author jumps around in time like this, she or he must give clues to help the reader understand what is happening. Often these clues are *time qualifiers*.

When you are reading or listening to a story, pay attention to the *time qualifiers*. They can help you understand what happened and when it happened. This helps you to follow the story better.

22

DAY 2

1. Read *Finding Clues To The Timing* (page 22). Discuss briefly. You may want to review the *time qualifiers* from DAY 1.

    3-5 minutes

Directions: In the story below, underline the time qualifiers. Then number the events listed on page 24 in the order in which they happened. Number the first event #1, the second event #2, and so on.

The skies were heavy with thick gray clouds. It was only three o'clock. Still early, Nick thought, he'd have plenty of time to get home. Earlier this morning Nick had listened to the weather report. The weather people had predicted a major snowstorm. From the looks of the sky, he was sure that the prediction would come true.

Nick was excited. He loved the snow. The prospect of walking home in the snowstorm bothered him not at all. He was well bundled and had just a little less than a mile to go. The path through the woods was completely clear. If it did snow, it would be the first snow of the season.

After Nick had been walking for about ten minutes, thick flakes began to swirl around him. Long ago, when he was in preschool, his teacher had told the class that each flake that fell from the sky was different. Ever since then, Nick had tried to find two flakes that were exactly alike, He hadn't found them yet, but he was sure that of the millions that fell from the sky, if he kept looking, ne would find the magical pair. He'd always told himself that when he found them, he would get whatever he'd wish for.

Nick was so busy catching and examining the lovely flakes that he didn't notice that the storm was intensifying. The swirling flakes had gathered force. The forest path was now a line of white winding through the tall pines. But Nick was not concentrating on the gathering forces of the snow. He was mesmerized by the thought of finding the two identical flakes. He stopped in his favorite spot, a clearing beneath two sycamore trees, so that he would have more light to examine the snow.

By the time he gave some attention to what was happening around him, the snow had become thick. It was so thick, in fact, that he could barely make out the outline of the trees around the clearing. He became a bit alarmed as he remembered his mother telling him, "Nick, this will be our first winter here. The storms in these parts come up quickly. You don't get the same warning as we did back east. Soon the ground is covered, and you can't see your hand in front of your face."

At the time Nick thought his mother was being a bit over-cautious. Not even here in the midwest could a storm sneak up that quickly on a boy who had experienced snowstorms all his life. But as Nick searched for the path that should now continue through a grove of maples, he knew his mother had been right to warn him.

Continued on page 24.

23

2. Have your students do Exercise III (pages 23-24) on their own, or read it aloud to them. We recommend that you read it aloud if you feel that your students can benefit from more practice in using the listening skills introduced in the first two units or if you think they would find the reading itself too cumbersome. When your students have completed the exercise, go over it with the class, first discussing the order of events in the story and then reviewing the time qualifiers in the passage.

15-20 minutes

Still he wasn't worried. He was very close to home after all, and the snow was just beginning to cover the ground. He did, however, quicken his pace. In his haste and because the snow made the forest a new, strange world, Nick took the wrong turn. He had gone half a mile when he discovered that he was heading toward the pond, not the old farmhouse that his family had moved into last summer.

The storm was lashing out in all its fury. Nick couldn't see the nose in front of his face, much less his hand. The maple and ash trees no longer protected the winding path. Now Nick was worried. He raced in what he thought was the right direction. It was getting dark. Soon he would not even have the comfort of daylight.

"Whatever am I going to do?" thought Nick as he admitted to himself that he didn't know if he was heading home or in some wild circle towards the pond. He was growing tired, and he realized that he'd have to catch his breath and think clearly before going on. He pulled his parka away from his watch to see how much time he would have left before total darkness was upon him. Instead of looking at his watch, he saw, wide-eyed, two snow flakes that for all the world looked perfectly alike. Here was the chance to test his theory.

"Oh, I wish I could find my way home!"

Just then, his dog, Monster, bounded into his arms. He was a great German shepherd with an amazing sense of direction. Nick knew now he had found his way home.

a. _____ Nick's family moved from the East.

b. _____ The weather people had predicted a snowstorm.

c. _____ Nick's mother had warned him about midwestern snowstorms.

d. _____ Nick's preschool teacher had told him no two snowflakes were alike.

e. _____ The storm was intensifying.

f. _____ Nick noticed the powerful storm.

g. _____ Nick was looking for a pair of identical snowflakes.

h. _____ It was three o'clock in the afternoon.

i. _____ Nick's dog, Monster, found him.

j. _____ Nick had taken the wrong turn.

24

PREDICTING OUTCOMES

When you are reading or listening to a story, you can use *time qualifiers* to help you understand the sequence of events. Then when you know what has already happened, you can often figure out what will happen next in the story.

Figuring out what will probably happen next is called *predicting outcomes*. When you predict an outcome, you use what you already know about a story to make a "good guess" about what will happen next.

Trying to *predict outcomes* also helps you to become actively involved in whatever you're hearing or reading.

When you predict an outcome, you ask yourself questions and try to answer them before you read or are told what happens.

EXERCISE IV

Directions: Read the paragraphs below and on pages 26-27. Circle the *time qualifiers* that help you to think about the possible outcome of each story. Then answer the question(s) that follows each paragraph.

1. When I awoke this morning, the sun was shining brightly in a clear, blue sky. I was excited because this was the day I had planned for the big picnic. After breakfast I turned on the radio and heard the weather report: "A moist cold front will be traveling rapidly across the Pacific Northwest. This front will push out the high currently settled over our region and will bring heavy rain. Rains will continue into tomorrow..." When I looked at the mountain to the west, I saw billowing black clouds.

Do you think this person will have a picnic on this day? What makes you think this?

_____

_____

_____

_____

25

3. Read *Predicting Outcomes* (page 25) aloud to your students, or have a student or students read it aloud. Discuss for clarity and emphasis.

   5 minutes

4. Read the directions for Exercise IV (pages 25-27) aloud to your students, and have them begin the exercise. Circulate among your students as they work on their predictions. Help them to figure out ways to make predictions. Stress that there is no right or wrong answer.

   10-15 minutes

5. Go over Exercise IV as a class. Discuss the students' predictions. The read the *Summary* (page 28) aloud.

   10 minutes

2. My teacher asked me to do an experiment to prove that a vacuum, or empty space, can't exist if there is something available to fill it. I knew that a candle needed oxygen to burn, and I also knew that oxygen took up space. So I put a candle in a shallow bowl and put an inch of water into the bowl. When I put a glass jar over the candle, I knew the candle would go out after it had used up all the oxygen within the jar. Then, with all the oxygen gone, the empty space within the jar would need to be filled, if possible, with another substance.

Predict what will happen to the water in the bowl. Explain your prediction.

_____

_____

_____

3. They say that if you don't learn from your mistakes, then "history will repeat itself." I never knew what that meant until I figured out there was a reason why I kept turning up on the "lost list." The first time I got lost, I had an excuse: I was only five years old. My mother had said, "Stay right here while Mama tries this dress on." I didn't listen to her. Instead I followed a cart full of toys. I should have learned to listen from that experience, but I didn't. I was seven when the teacher told our class to report to the auditorium after lunch. Again I wasn't listening, so I spent the better part of the afternoon looking for my class. When it finally came time for our class trip to Montreal, I was really excited. I was also determined not to get lost, but as I said, "History has a way of repeating itself."

Do you think the writer gets lost in Montreal? Why do you think the way you do?

_____

_____

_____

26

4. In 1641 the population of New France was 240. Most of the people living there were single soldiers. French officials asked unmarried women to come to the New World to become soldiers' wives. Ships soon arrived in New France carrying more than 150 female immigrants. Then the government offered special rewards for large families. If people had ten children, they received a pension. Girls were given large sums if they married before they were sixteen. Boys who married before the age of twenty also received special rewards.

Predict the population of New France in 1675. What makes you think this?

_____

_____

_____

_____

27

UNIT III SUMMARY: GETTING THE TIMING DOWN

"Getting the timing down" means understanding the order of events in a story. The order in which things take place in a story is also called the *sequence* of events.

When you read or listen to a story, you can recognize key words that tell you about when events take place. These words are called *time qualifiers*. Some examples of time qualifiers are these: after, before, until, while, following, during.

You can use your ability to "get the timing down" to understand when things happen in a story and to *predict outcomes*. This means to use what you already know about the sequence of events in a story to figure out what will probably happen next. By trying to predict outcomes as you read or listen, you can become a more active and involved reader or listener.

28

ANSWERS FOR EXERCISES IN UNIT III

Pages 18-19: Exercise I

a. __5__ Chuck's

b. __4__ Theater

c. __8__ Donna's Kennels

d. __1__ FB Garage

e. __9__ Home

f. __3__ Wellington Field

g. __7__ C.T.'s Daycare

h. __6__ Library

i. __2__ Dorie's Cookie Factory

Page 21: Exercise II

(Before) Molly left for school, she ate two pieces of toast.

We set up the tents (while) the others gathered firewood.

1. I had a great time (after) I got to know all the people there.

2. (Before) Miguel had realized the danger he was in, he was enjoying sailing over the waves.

3. Darcy searched for clues to the disappearance of her brother, Ted, but (in the meantime,) he slept soundly, unaware that she was trying to find him.

4. It had taken years of hard work, but (finally) the statue was finished.

5. (Following) the wedding ceremony, there was a reception at the Martin Luther King Community Center.

6. Water expands (when) it is cooled.

7. (As) the masses drew back, they carved lakes and hills upon the earth's surface.

8. <u>Divide the money equally among yourselves,</u> and (then) go to the store.

9. <u>The water pressure built up</u> (until) the dam finally cracked.

10. All (during) the time I had been outdoors planting, the baby had been playing happily in her pen.

Pages 23-24; Exercise III

The skies were heavy with thick gray clouds. It was only three o'clock. <u>Still early,</u> Nick thought, he'd have plenty of time to get home. <u>Earlier</u> this morning Nick had listened to the weather report. The weather people had predicted a major snowstorm. From the looks of the sky, he was sure that the prediction would come true.

Nick was excited. He loved the snow. The prospect of walking home in the snowstorm bothered him not at all. He was well bundled and had just a little less than a mile to go. The path through the woods was completely clear. If it did snow, it would be the first snow of the season.

<u>After</u> Nick had been walking for about ten minutes, thick flakes began to swirl around him. <u>Long ago,</u> when he was in pre-school, his teacher had told the class that each flake that fell from the sky was different. <u>Ever since then,</u> Nick had tried to find two flakes that were exactly alike. He hadn't found them yet, but he was sure that of the millions that fell from the sky, if he kept looking, he would find the magical pair. He'd always told himself that when he found them, he would get whatever he'd wish for.

Nick was so busy catching and examining the lovely flakes that he didn't notice that the storm was intensifying. The swirling flakes had gathered force. The forest path was now a line of white winding through the tall pines. But Nick was not concentrating on the gathering forces of the snow. He was mesmerized by the thought of finding the two identical flakes. He stopped in his favorite spot, a clearing beneath two sycamore trees, so that he would have more light to examine the snow.

<u>By the time</u> he gave some attention to what was happening around him, the snow had become thick. It was so thick, in fact, that he could barely make out the outline of the trees around the clearing. He became a bit alarmed as he remembered his mother telling him, "Nick, this will be our first winter here. The storms in these parts come up quickly. You don't get the same warning as we did back east. <u>Soon</u> the ground is covered, and you can't see your hand in front of your face."

<u>At the time</u> Nick thought his mother was being a bit over-cautious. Not even here in the midwest could a storm sneak up that quickly on a boy who had experienced snowstorms all his life. But as Nick searched for the path that should now continue through a grove of maples, he knew his mother had been right to warn him.

Still he wasn't worried. He was very close to home after all, and the snow was just beginning to cover the ground. He did, however, quicken his pace. In his haste and because the snow made the forest a new, strange world, Nick took the wrong turn. He had gone half a mile <u>when</u> he discovered that he was heading toward the pond, not the old farmhouse that his family had moved into last summer.

The storm was lashing out in all its fury. Nick couldn't see the nose in front of his face, much less his hand. The maple and ash trees no longer protected the winding path. <u>Now</u> Nick was worried. He raced in what he thought was the right direction. It was getting dark. <u>Soon</u> he would not even have the comfort of daylight.

"Whatever am I going to do?" thought Nick as he admitted to himself that he didn't know if he was heading home or in some wild circle towards the pond. He was growing tired, and he realized that he'd have to catch his breath and think clearly <u>before</u> going on. He pulled his parka away from his watch to see how much time he would have left <u>before</u> total darkness was upon him. Instead of looking at his watch, he saw, wide-eyed, two snow flakes that for all the world looked perfectly alike. Here was the chance to test his theory.

"Oh, I wish I could find my way home!"

<u>Just then</u>, his dog, Monster, bounded into his arms. He was a great German shepherd with an amazing sense of direction. Nick knew <u>now</u> he had found his way home.

a. ___2___

b. ___4___

c. ___3___

d. ___1___

e. ___7___

f. ___8___

g. ___6___

h. ___5___

i. ___10___

j. ___9___

Pages 25-27: Exercise IV

Answers will vary. Accept any answer that makes sense. You may want to work out #4 together. There is no "right" formula, but you will want to keep the following details in mind:

— 150 women were shipped in 1641. Probably all of them married.

— Discuss what the average number of children may have been per family. Multiply that average by 150. This will give you a starting point. Figure that half of these children were girls and would produce more children.

— The first year women could produce children would be 1642. The first of these children would probably start having children in 1657 as the first child would then be fifteen years old. In another fifteen years, the grandchildren would start having children.

— This activity would be a good one to diagram or map on the board.

ADDITIONAL SUGGESTIONS

1. Develop ways in which your students can use their sequencing skills as a part of your regular curriculum. The more experience that your students have in working with the sequences, the more competent they will become in employing these skills. Some of the ways you can do this are the following:

a. Write out flow charts for certain class procedures.

Afternoon Recess in Grade 6

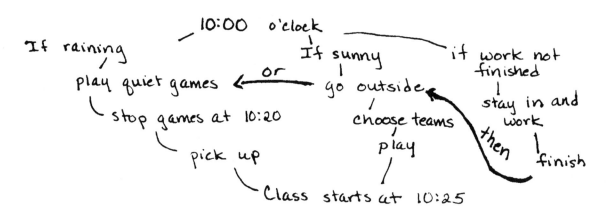

Suggest other activities that lend themselves to the use of flow charts, such as revising written work, choosing a spelling team, figuring out why a science experiment didn't work and restructuring the experiment, and so on. In working with sequencing focus your students' attention on the "stable points" in a sequence: beginnings and ends, events which are directly connected, and obvious "befores" and "afters."

b. Read a novel to your class. Read for a certain amount of time each day. At the end of each reading, discuss the clues that will structure the events of the next reading. Invite your students to predict what could happen.

You will want to choose novels that are interesting to your class as well as novels that have a well developed sequence of events. Some great resources for novel and short story suggestions are:

Best Books for Children by Valerie Lewis and Walter Mayes (Avon Books, 1998)
Teaching with Caldecott Books: Activities across the Curriculum by C. Moen (Scholastic, 1991)
Hey! Listen to This: Stories to Read Aloud by Jim Trelease (Penguin, 1992)
Great Books for Boys 2-14 and *Great Books for Girls 2-14* by Kathleen O'Dean (Ballantine, 1997, 1998)

c. Suggest some formulas for writing factual responses. These can be helpful when the students want to prove a point or stage a discussion. Such formulas might look like this:

I think television is harmful/helpful to me as a person who is learning a lot about the world now. In the first place the most important thing about watching television is _____

_____

_____

Then, you must consider that television_____

_____

_____

In addition to the examples listed above, television can be_____

_____

_____

In summary I would like to stress that television_____

_____

_____

You will want to be careful not to overuse these formulas as they apply best to certain subject matter and learning styles. Many students can be inhibited by too much formulated writing. It is also well worth the time and effort spent to help students generate the formulas themselves.

2. Time qualifiers can provide students with one kind of clue in recognizing and understanding sequences. *Connectors* offer another kind of clue. *Connectors* are words that connect ideas together. They can tell you that some action or event has already taken place. They can also inform you about sequences not in time but in the organization of a passage. For example, in the following sentence, *another one* is a connector: Another one of the Fox's clever tricks was flattery.

Introduce the idea of *connectors* to your students. Then have them read a passage in which the paragraphs are out of the correct order, like the one below. Ask your students to circle the *connectors* in these paragraphs and then place the paragraphs in the correct order by numbering them.

_____ Another woman who tricked the British was Dicey Langston of South Carolina. She was only fifteen when she became a self-appointed spy. She would watch British military maneuvers from her farm and report to the Patriots. The British were slow to realize that a young girl was the source of so many information leaks.

_____ One of the underestimated women was Nancy Hart. British soldiers burst into her home demanding to be fed. She sent her daughter next door to get some water and warn the Patriots. By the time the Patriots arrived with her daughter, Nancy Hart had stolen the British rifles, killed one soldier, and cornered the rest of them.

_____ At the time of the Revolutionary War, most people expected women to remain quiet, obedient, and in the background of manly pursuits. This idea got many British soldiers in trouble because these soldiers underestimated the strength and cunning of American women.

_____ Probably the most famous of all women Patriots was Deborah Sampson. Unlike the other two women mentioned, she didn't set out to fool the British by appearing to be a weak female. She dressed herself as a man and fought for three years in the army. Her identity was discovered only when she needed to be nursed for a high fever. She was then dismissed, for even the Patriots underestimated the power of a fighting woman.

3. The following student workbooks suggest some excellent activities that stress sequencing:

   Action and Adventures; Mystery and Suspense; Myths and Fables by Judith B. Steffens and Judy F. Carr (The Learning Works, 1985).

4. Take newspaper articles or stories from workbooks. Cut them up, and code them in a way that will allow you to put them together. Then mount them on cardboard so that they can withstand some handling. Give four stories to a group of three to four students. Mix up the cards. Challenge the group to put the story parts in the correct pile as well as the correct sequence.

5. Give your students the end of a story such as the following:

   A man was found dead in what appeared to be a poorly dug, shallow ditch.

   Challenge your students to discover the rest of the story by asking you questions. Explain that they may only ask questions that can be answered by "yes" or "no." Also note that they must listen carefully to each other's questions and your answers.

   Your students will ask questions that explore various story threads, or sequences, until they can reconstruct the entire story.

   The remainder of the story begun above is the following:

   A man was hiking in early spring. He had not paid any attention to the avalanche warnings that the park had posted. He wandered off into a danger zone where a huge boulder rolled down the mountain at a tremendous speed, carving a path as it went. The boulder hit him, and he was killed instantaneously.

6. Another approach to sequencing is to use *Sequencing — Basic Skill Series* by Claire Norman (Instructional Fair, Inc., 1999).

UNIT IV: A MATTER OF TIME

The activities in this unit help your students begin to understand how they make sense of time and how they can begin to control their own use of time through planning. This unit will give you a greater awareness of how your students perceive time.

Some of your students will probably enjoy making and using a schedule. Others may not. We suggest that you introduce your students to the idea of a schedule as a tool for one's own use, not as an obligation that one does for others. We have found that setting this unit within such a framework can help to lessen any resistance that your students feel about learning how to make and use a schedule.

UNIT IV: A MATTER OF TIME

INTRODUCTION

Think about the meaning of the word *time*. Can you give a definition for this word? Does this word have more than one meaning for you?

Write your definition for the word *time* on the lines below. If you can think of more than one definition, write two or three.

time: _____

_____

_____

_____

_____

_____

_____

You may have found it difficult to define the word *time*. Time is not something that we can touch, see, or smell. Yet we can "feel" time or sense it as it passes. And we can also "hear" time or sense the order in a piece of music.

Our sense of time seems to change as we grow older. For instance, now you'd probably think that you're wasting your time if you were perfectly healthy and spent a whole day in bed. When you were a baby, however, you were usually content to lie in bed, asleep and awake, for most of the day and night.

This unit will help you to look more carefully at what time is and how you use your time.

29

SUGGESTED DIRECTIONS FOR UNIT V

PLEASE NOTE: This unit will require two 40 minute class periods.

DAY 1

1. You will want to read through this unit carefully before you teach it. If you have a young class, you may want to have your students do *Making A Schedule* (pages 39-41) as a group. If you choose this option, pick an appropriate class project prior to this class. Then lead your students through *Making a Schedule* in relation to the class project.

2. The exercises on pages 40-41 require students to use pencils. If they don't have their own, you will have to provide them.

3. Have your students read the *Introduction* (page 29) and write their definition(s). Discuss the various definitions of "time."

    Approximate time: 15 minutes

4. Divide your class into small groups of 3-4 students. Tell them they will do Exercise I (pages 30-31) individually but will discuss it in their groups. Read the directions for Exercise I aloud. Also call your students' attention to the additional directions at the bottom of page 31. Ask your students to do Exercise I. Tell them that when all the group members have finished the exercise, they should tell each other which events they have starred and discuss their agreements and disagreements.

15 minutes

TIME LINE: MY LIFE

YEAR	YEAR IN MY LIFE	EVENTS IN MY LIFE
	0	I was born.
	1	
	2	
	3	
	4	
	5	
	6	
	7	
	8	
	9	I was nine years old.
	10	
	11	
	12	
	13	
	14	
	15	
	16	
	17	

Now put a star in front of each event that you think happened in the lives of all the other people in your class during the same YEAR IN MY LIFE. (It does not have to be the same calendar YEAR.)

31

76

EXERCISE II

Directions: Sometimes it's important for us to know if events happened before or after other events.

Arrange each group of events below according to when you think they happened. Which happened first? Put a #1 in the blank before the event that happened first. Put a #2 in the blank before the event that happened next, and so on up to #4.

REMEMBER: The event that happened first is the one that took place *the longest time ago*.

GROUP A

_____ Television was invented.

_____ Radio was invented.

_____ The personal computer was invented.

_____ The horsedrawn wagon was invented.

GROUP B

_____ Neil Armstrong first walked on the moon.

_____ Columbus sailed to America.

_____ The automobile was invented.

_____ Betsy Ross stitched together the first American flag.

GROUP C

_____ People first invented language.

_____ George Washington was elected the first President of the United States.

_____ The Egyptians built the pyramids.

_____ My teacher was born.

32

5. Have a student or students read the directions for Exercise II (page 32) aloud. Have your students do the exercise. Then go over it as a class.

8-10 minutes

A STRING OF EVENTS—PLANNING THE STEPS

When you have a certain project in mind such as making a shirt, building a shelf, or getting a book report ready for school, you often think through the things you need to do—or steps you need to take—to complete the project. What's the first step? The second one? And so on.

For instance, if you want to do your book report, you think about all the things that need to be done before you can write a final draft. Some of those things might be:

read the book
discuss the book with your teacher
outline the main events
outline the main characters
write a rough draft

You must have a clear idea of the project you wish to do. You must also think of the steps you need to take in order to get this project done. It is helpful to think of these steps as a *string of events*. In other words, all the steps you take and the order in which you take them must have a logical connection. You can't outline the main events of the book until you have read the book.

EXERCISE III

Directions: Look at the Example below and events 1-3 on page 34. The steps that are listed below them are not in the correct order.

Suggest a better order by numbering the first thing to be done as #1, and the second thing as #2, and so on.

Example: Make pancakes

a. _____ mix ingredients
b. _____ heat skillet
c. _____ read recipe
d. _____ eat pancakes
e. _____ find recipe
f. _____ get out necessary ingredients
g. _____ put mixture in hot, greased skillet
h. _____ flip pancakes

33

DAY 2

1. Have a student or students read aloud *A String of Events—Planning the Steps* (page 33), or read it aloud yourself. Discuss briefly.

5 minutes

2. Read over the directions to Exercise III (pages 33-34) with your class. Do the example together. You might want to do this exercise as a class activity. If you have the students do this exercise in small groups or individually, give them time to complete it. Then have them share their answers. Discuss as feels helpful.

8-12 minutes

1. Change the tire on my bicycle

a. _____ take out the old tube
b. _____ blow up the new tube
c. _____ check inside tire for anything that might puncture new tube
d. _____ take off tire
e. _____ put in new tube
f. _____ put tire back on

2. Make a stuffed pillow

a. _____ sew the pieces together
b. _____ fill the pillow with polyester fill
c. _____ pick out a design
d. _____ cut out the pattern pieces
e. _____ pick out the materials
f. _____ leave an open seam for filling
g. _____ stitch up open seam

3. Plan to see a movie

a. _____ call friend
b. _____ check available movies in the newspaper
c. _____ suggest going to a movie together
d. _____ check to see if I have enough money
e. _____ get permission from parents
f. _____ arrange transportation to see movie

34

EXERCISE IV

Directions: Now look at the tasks below and on page 36. Create a string of events for doing the tasks below. Write the events on the lines provided.

Example

Make a bacon, lettuce, and tomato sandwich

1. check to see if I have ingredients
2. fry the bacon
3. wash the lettuce-set it on towel to dry
4. cut tomatoes
5. drain fat from bacon
6. toast bread
7. put mayonnaise on toast
8. layer the bacon, lettuce, and tomato on toast
9. put on top of sandwich
10. cut sandwich in half
11. eat

Make a paper mache mask

_____

_____

_____

_____

_____

_____

_____

_____

_____

_____

_____

35

3. Read aloud the directions to Exercise IV (pages 35-36). Have the students complete this activity individually or in small groups. When they have done so, ask the students to share their answers. Discuss as feels helpful.

8-12 minutes

Put a young child to bed

_____

_____

_____

_____

_____

_____

_____

_____

_____

_____

Study for a spelling quiz

_____

_____

_____

_____

_____

_____

_____

_____

_____

_____

36

WHAT IS A SCHEDULE?

As you grow older, you begin to think more about the "string" of events in your life: what will happen tomorrow, and the next day, and so on. As you do, you'll want to be able to plan some of the events ahead of time.

When you are trying to plan ahead, it can be helpful to make a *schedule* for yourself. A *schedule is a plan for what you want to do in the future.*

Usually when you plan, you "string" things that need to happen backwards. That is, *first* you decide what your goal is. Then you figure out how you can reach it.

For instance, you might be thinking of the goal of having a Friday evening pizza party. The pizza party is the last thing that will happen in the string. Some of the steps you have to take before the party are these:

    ask your parents for permission
    save your allowance
    invite your friends
    buy the paper goods
    buy drinks
    clean the party room
    borrow some CDs to play
    order the pizza
    pick up the pizza

When you do this kind of planning, a *schedule* helps you to understand what the steps are to reach your goal and when you need to do them. Look at the sample *schedule* on page 38 for *Planning My Pizza Party.*

37

4. Have a student or students read aloud *What Is A Schedule?* (page 37), or read it aloud yourself. Discuss briefly.

   3-5 minutes

WEEKLY SCHEDULE	Day 1 Saturday	Day 2 Sunday	Day 3 Monday	Day 4 Tuesday	Day 5 Wednesday	Day 6 Thursday	Day 7 Friday
Morning — Before School	Ask parents for permission						
Mid-Day — During School			Invite friends that I didn't call	Ask friends to bring Cds			
Late Afternoon — After School	Babysit to earn money	Call friends to invite them	Get allowance DON'T SPEND IT!	Call friends I didn't see to bring Cds		Go shopping: paper goods other munchies drinks cups	Set up for party Order Pizza Pick up Pizza
Evening — After Dinner						Clean party room	PARTY!

Schedule for Planning My Pizza Party

EXERCISE V

MAKING A SCHEDULE

Directions: 1. Choose something you would really like to do from the goals listed below, or think of your own goal.

Circle the goal of your choice if it's one of the goals listed below. If it isn't, write your goal on the line below the list.

learn a computer program

plan a _____ party

get a book report done

get a school project done

make a new friend

build a model (airplane, car, boat, etc.)

finish a sewing project

My goal is _____

2. Now make a list of steps – or a string of events – that have to be done before your goal is accomplished.

_____

_____

_____

_____

_____

_____

_____

_____

_____

_____

_____

_____

Continued on page 40.

39

5. Read aloud the directions to Exercise V: *Making a Schedule* (pages 39-40). If you have decided to complete this exercise as a class, discuss the daily set up of the schedule. Although the steps to doing the project will be the same, individuals will have to decide how the daily schedule can work for them.

If you have your students do this exercise individually, ask them to read the instructions and carefully examine the *Planning My Pizza Party* sample schedule (page 38). Discuss for emphasis and clarification. When you have completed the discussion, have your students begin to create their schedules. As they work, circulate around the room, answering questions and offering helpful suggestions.

If there is time, have your students complete their schedules. If not, have them complete their schedules for homework.

15-20 minutes

3. On *My Schedule* on page 41, write tomorrow's day of the week in the blank below Day 1. Then write in the rest of the days of the week on your schedule.

4. Think about when you want to do the first step that you have listed above. When you have decided when to do that step, write the step into the correct box on *My Schedule*. Do the same for all the other steps that lead to your goal. *BE SURE TO WRITE YOUR SCHEDULE IN PENCIL!* If you write in pencil, you'll be able to make changes in your schedule if you need to do so.

> *REMEMBER:* When you plan to work on your project during a block of time, that doesn't mean you'll spend all of that time working on your project. It means you'll spend at least some time on your project.
>
> For example, let's say that you plan to work on a step during Tuesday evening after dinner and write that into your schedule. This means that you intend to spend at least some time on your step during Tuesday evening.

5. When you have finished making your schedule for the goal you have chosen, look carefully at what you have planned. Does it seem reasonable to you? Is this a plan that will work for you? If not, change it.

40

6. Have your students make a copy of their schedule for homework and hand it in to you the next day. Go over the schedules, and give your students constructive feedback. *Then ask your students to use their schedules to achieve their goal during the next week.*

WEEKLY SCHEDULE	Day 1	Day 2	Day 3	Day 4	Day 5	Day 6	Day 7
Morning — Before School							
Mid-Day — During School							
Late Afternoon — After School							
Evening — After Dinner							

41

My Schedule

86

USING YOUR SCHEDULE: WHAT HAPPENED?

How well did your schedule work for you? Think about the questions below, and then answer them.

1. Did I get everything done that I wanted to do?

   _____

2. Did anything get in the way of my schedule? If things did get in the way, what were they?

   _____

   _____

   _____

3. How could I make a more useful schedule?

   _____

   _____

4. How does making plans seem helpful to me?

   _____

   _____

5. How does making plans seem not helpful to me?

   _____

   _____

42

7. The day after the end of the scheduled week, ask your students to do *Using Your Schedule: What Happened?* (page 42). Discuss your students' experiences with their schedules in class.

UNIT IV SUMMARY: A MATTER OF TIME

Making a *schedule* for yourself can be helpful when you're trying to plan ahead. A *schedule* is a plan for what you want to do in the future.

When you're making a schedule, first think about what you want to do or the goal you want to accomplish. Then think about all the steps you have to take to reach that goal.

Write into your schedule *when* you plan to work and *what* you plan to get done each time that you work.

When you finish making your schedule, look it over carefully. Does it seem reasonable for you? If not, change it.

After you use your schedule, think about how well it worked for you. Was your schedule helpful? If it wasn't helpful, how could you make a more useful schedule?

43

ANSWERS FOR EXERCISES IN UNIT IV

Pages 30-31: Exercise I

Answers will vary.

Page 32: Exercise II

Group A

  3
  2
  4
  1

Group B

  4
  2
  3
  1

Group C

  1
  3
  2
  4

Pages 33-34: Exercise III

Answers may vary.

Example

a. 4
b. 5
c. 2
d. 8
e. 1
f. 3
g. 6
h. 7

1.

a. __2__

b. __5__

c. __3__

d. __1__

e. __4__

f. __6__

2.

a. __4__

b. __6__

c. __1__

d. __3__

e. __2__

f. __5__

g. __7__

3.

a. __4__

b. __3__

c. __5__

d. __1__

e. __2__

f. __6__

g. __7__

Pages 35-36: Exercise IV

Answers will vary.

ADDITIONAL SUGGESTIONS

1. Provide your students with at least one structured experience in making and using a schedule beyond the exercises in this unit. Assign a project for your class. Ask your students to draw up a schedule for completion of the project. Then let them go ahead and work on the project. When your students hand in their completed projects, also ask them to evaluate their own schedules and how useful they were in completing the work of the project.

2. Post a large calendar with school and class deadlines. You may also want to get smaller copies of the same calendar for three-ring binders. Encourage students to write in their own deadlines and important activities.

3. Have your students interview the adults in various professions to see how they schedule their time. Have them report to the class the various systems of scheduling that they discover. Encourage them to try ways of scheduling that are interesting to them.

4. Make a collection of commercial calendars/planners of various sorts and sizes. Invite your students to peruse them, and discuss with your students how and why different formats serve different uses for these planners.

5. If your school does not have a common school planner, engage your students in designing a calendar/planner for sale in your school.

UNIT V: PUTTING IDEAS TOGETHER

Putting ideas together or categorization is an important foundation skill. First we need to help our students learn to see the interrelatedness of detail before we can expect them to develop the skills involved in relating concepts.

Observe your students as they read an assigned text. You may be surprised to discover that many read without trying to organize the information in their reading in any way. To help our students learn to understand the relations between categories and their parts, we need to teach them the necessary skills.

This unit provides an initial experience in learning the skill of categorization. It also helps your students to learn how they can remember information more effectively when it is organized into categories.

SUGGESTED DIRECTIONS FOR UNIT V

PLEASE NOTE: In its entirety, this unit requires two 40 minute class periods. However we urge you to read over all the directions carefully and tailor the unit to your class. You may want to omit the repetition of Exercise I, especially if you have an older class. For a younger class, you may want to omit some or all of Exercise III, which deals with higher levels of categorization. You'll want to include Exercise IV with either kind of class.

DAY 1

1. Before you teach this unit, make enough copies of each list below for half of your class. (PLEASE NOTE: You may want to replace Lists C & D with lists that include categories generated from your own curriculum.)

List A

basketball	duck	robin	tennis
hen	frisbee	green	football
red	tulip	daisy	blue
swan	pink	purple	daffodil
long jump	rose	lilac	raven

List B

SPORTS	BIRDS	COLORS	FLOWERS
basketball	duck	pink	daisy
long jump	hen	purple	rose
frisbee	robin	red	lilac
tennis	swan	green	tulip
football	raven	blue	daffodil

List C

alligator	ladybug	lizard	goat
catfish	horse	dog	snake
cat	goldfish	cow	chameleon
gnat	fly	shark	caterpillar
tuna	shark	mosquito	crocodile

List D

MAMMALS	REPTILES	FISH	INSECTS
cow	alligator	trout	fly
horse	snake	tuna	gnat
dog	lizard	goldfish	ladybug
cat	chameleon	shark	mosquito
goat	crocodile	catfish	caterpillar

93

2. Briefly introduce this unit orally. Tell your students that you are going to start the unit with an exercise. Pass out List A to one half of the class, List B to the other half. Don't let your students know that there are two separate lists. Instruct your students to study the words on their list and try to remember as many as possible. Tell them that they will have only five minutes to do this.

After five minutes, collect the lists. Ask your students to open their **Student Texts** to page 44 and write down all the words they can remember in the spaces provided. Allow about two minutes for this.

Approximate time: 10 minutes

UNIT V: PUTTING IDEAS TOGETHER

EXERCISE I

Directions: List all of the words that you can remember from the list of words your teacher gave you.

_____ _____ _____ _____

_____ _____ _____ _____

_____ _____ _____ _____

_____ _____ _____ _____

_____ _____ _____ _____

Directions: Try it again. This time you will have looked at a list that has been organized differently.

_____ _____ _____ _____

_____ _____ _____ _____

_____ _____ _____ _____

_____ _____ _____ _____

_____ _____ _____ _____

44

3. Check to see which half of the class remembered the most words. (Studies show that people can remember more effectively when ideas or pieces of information are organized into categories.) Most likely the students with List B (and later List D) will remember more words. Discuss the outcome in your class briefly.

    5 minutes

4. If you choose, repeat the exercise with Lists C and D or lists that you have generated.

    15 minutes

WHY DO YOU ORGANIZE INFORMATION?

When you organize information or ideas, you can discover how the various pieces of information or ideas relate to each other. Also you can usually remember information and ideas better when you organize them.

HOW DO YOU ORGANIZE INFORMATION?

Each word in the lists that your teacher gave you is a piece of information. Each time you tried the exercise above, half of you had a list in which the words were organized into *categories*.

A *category* is a name for a group of ideas or pieces of information that have something in common. For example, *birds* is a category. Duck, hen, robin, swan, and raven all fit into the category of *birds*.

Putting ideas and information into categories is a good way to organize your ideas and information. It will help you to remember them better and to understand how the ideas and information are similar and how they are different.

EXAMPLE

Directions: Look at the following group of words. Then answer the questions below it.

Louisiana	Toronto	New Jersey
Los Angeles	New Mexico	New York

1. Which word(s) fits into the category of *cities*? _____

_____

2. Which word(s) fits into the category of *words ending in vowels*? _____

_____

3. Which word(s) does *not* fit into the category of places in the United States?

_____

4. Name a category in which all of these words fit.

_____

45

---

5. Read *Why Do You Organize Information?* and *How Do You Organize Information?* (page 45) aloud. Discuss briefly.

   5 minutes

6. Go over the *Example* (page 45) orally. Then have your students start Exercise II (pages 46-49) individually or in pairs. Ask them to do as much of the exercise as they can in the time remaining. Have them complete this exercise for homework.

   20-25 minutes

EXERCISE II

Directions: Look at the words in Group A. Then answer the questions below it. Do the same for Groups B-D on pages 47-49.

GROUP A

ocean	lake	stream
river	mountain	sea

1. Which word(s) fits into the category of *bodies of water*? _____

    _____

2. Which word(s) can *not* be listed in the category of *words beginning with consonants*?

    _____

    _____

3. Which word(s) can be listed in the category of *items found on a map of your state*?

    _____

    _____

4. Name a category in which all of these words fit.

    _____

46

DAY 2

1. Go over Exercise II orally. Discuss any categories that gave the students difficulty.

    7-10 minutes

GROUP B

wet	cold	green
dark	dry	hot

5. Which word(s) probably fits into the category of *words used to describe a desert*?

   _____

6. Which word(s) probably fits into the category of *words used to describe winter at the North Pole*?

   _____

7. Which word(s) fits into the category of *words that describe temperatures*?

   _____

8. Name a category in which all of these words fit.

   _____

empress	doctor	king
president	mechanic	pilot

9. Which word(s) fits into the category of *occupations that only women can have?*

_____

10. Which word(s) fits into the category of *occupations that only men can have?*

_____

11. Which word(s) can *not* be found in the category of *leaders of countries?*

_____

12. Name a category in which all of these words fit.

_____

GROUP D

roots	stems	plants
leaves	seeds	green

13. Which word(s) does *not* fit into the category of *parts of plants*? _____

_____

14. Which word(s) fits into the category of *colors*? _____

_____

15. Which word(s) does *not* fit into the category of *words that have two vowels together that make a single sound*?

_____

_____

16. Name a category in which *none* of these words fits.

_____

EXERCISE III

Directions: Look at the words in Group E. Then answer the questions below it. Do the same for Groups F-L on pages 50-56.

For Groups H-L on pages 52-56, list the letters of phrases or sentences that you choose. You don't need to copy the phrase or sentence itself.

GROUP E

gasoline	wood	coal
water	air	steel

17. Which word(s) fits into the category of *things that will burn?* _____

_____

18. Which word(s) fits into the category of *liquids?* _____

_____

19. Which word(s) fits into the category of *metals?* _____

_____

20. Name a category in which all of these words fit.

_____

GROUP F

heart	feather	skin
fur	lung	scales

21. Which word(s) fits into the category of *things that are inside the bodies of animals?*

_____

22. Which word(s) fits into the category of *coverings that protect animals?*

_____

23. Which word(s) does *not* fit into the category of *parts of animals?*

_____

24. Name *two* categories in which all of these words fit.

_____

50

2.   Have your students do part or all of Exercise III (pages 50-56) individually or in pairs. Then go over the exercise in class. Discuss any of the categories that gave your students problems.

15-25 minutes

GROUP G

fraction	subtraction	addition
multiplication	calculator	computer

25. Which word(s) does *not* fit into the category of *mathematical terms*?

   _____

26. Which word(s) does *not* fit into the category of *machines*?

   _____

27. Which word(s) fits into the category of *words that have at least four syllables*?

   _____

28. Name two categories in which none of these words fits.

   _____

GROUP H

a. go to the store
b. mend the cuffs
c. fix bathroom faucet
d. pick up laundry
e. call Jane
f. write letters

29. Which phrase(s) fits into the category of *chores*? _____

_____

30. Which phrase(s) fits into the category of *errands*? _____

_____

31. Which phrase(s) fits into the category of *things to do in my free time*?

_____

32. Name a category in which all of these phrases fit.

_____

GROUP I

a. once upon a time
b. this little piggy
c. Christopher Robin
d. who's been sleeping in my bed?
e. not by the hair of my chinny chin chin
f. the little red hen

33. Which phrase(s) fits into the category of *characters from children's tales*?

   _____

34. Which phrase(s) fits into the category of *well known lines*?

   _____

35. Which phrase(s) fits into the category of *dialogue* (the words characters speak)?

   _____

36. Name a category in which all of these phrases fit.

   _____

53

104

GROUP J

a. examining animal characteristics and behavior
b. analyzing data gathered from telescope observation
c. finding cures for diseases
d. writing observations
e. collecting information
f. studying climate

37. Which phrase(s) fits into the category of *parts of a scientist's job?* _____

    _____

38. Which phrase(s) fits into the category of *ways that meteorologists* (scientists who study the weather) *make predictions*?

    _____

    _____

39. Which phrase(s) fits into the category of *part of an animal behaviorist's job*?

    _____

40. Name a category in which all of these phrases fit.

    _____

54

GROUP K

a. A small cottage stood alone in the dark woods.
b. King Midas wished that everything he touched would turn to gold.
c. The fox kept praising Chanticleer.
d. Midas's daughter was unaware that everything her father touched would turn to gold.
e. Chanticleer was a rooster who was overly proud of himself.
f. This pride eventually got the vain bird in trouble.
g. King Midas's beautiful castle and many riches were not enough.

41. Which sentence(s) fits into the category called "The Golden Touch"?

   _____

42. Which sentence(s) fits into the category called "The Fox and Chanticleer"?

   _____

43. Which sentence(s) fits into neither category?

   _____

44. Name a category in which all of these sentences fit.

   _____

55

106

GROUP L

a. Several Indian or Native American tribes populated the continent of North America before the arrival of white people.
b. When the Europeans invaded South America, they found many highly developed Native American civilizations.
c. The North American Indian tribes formed seven nations.
d. One of the most highly developed South American tribes was the Incas.
e. The Algonquin was one great Native American nation of Northeastern America.
f. The Inca tribe of South America was a part of a larger branch called the Quecha.
g. The Delaware tribe inhabited the region where Pennsylvania is today.

45. Which sentence(s) fits into the category of *Native Americans of North America*?

   _____

46. Which sentence(s) fits into the category of *South American Native Americans*?

   _____

47. Which of the sentences above would *not* fit into a category of Columbus's voyages?

   _____

48. Name a category in which all of these sentences fit.

   _____

56

107

EXERCISE IV

Directions: Organize the words below into as many categories as possible.

List the categories and the words grouped within them in the spaces below and on the following pages. You must list at least three words in each category that you create. You may use the same word in more than one category.

Try to create categories that no one else will!

star	see	lobster	crow
man	walnut	treasure	creator
wave	stove	woman	October
July	fox	mountain	pocket
loon	September	drummer	potato
cashew	strawberry	highway	volcano
earthquake	ax	hammer	hyena
empress	meteor	goat	stew
dunce	sponge	August	rat
octopus	river	ostrich	crater
wedge	June	saw	stone
fish	earth	ribbon	drill
valley	eel	November	onion
canary	hill	rake	whale

CATEGORY _____

Words _____

_____

_____

_____

CATEGORY _____

Words _____

_____

_____

_____

CATEGORY _____

Words _____

_____

_____

_____

CATEGORY _____

Words _____

_____

_____

_____

57

3. Divide the class into small groups of 3-4 students. Read the directions for Exercise IV (page 57) aloud, or have a student read them. Stress that there must be three words in each category. Tell the students that they will have ten minutes for this exercise. Then have them begin the exercise.

You can make this into a game by giving each group "a point" for each category it has created that is not mentioned by any other group.

After ten minutes go over Exercise IV in class. Have each group list its categories on the board. Discover which groups have created unique categories.

15-20 minutes

PLEASE NOTE: You may want to have your class continue Exercise IV on the following day so you can take more time with it.

CATEGORY _____   CATEGORY _____

Words _____   Words _____

_____   _____

_____   _____

_____   _____

_____   _____

CATEGORY _____   CATEGORY _____

Words _____   Words _____

_____   _____

_____   _____

_____   _____

_____   _____

CATEGORY _____   CATEGORY _____

Words _____   Words _____

_____   _____

_____   _____

_____   _____

_____   _____

CATEGORY _____   CATEGORY _____

Words _____   Words _____

_____   _____

_____   _____

_____   _____

_____   _____

CATEGORY _____   CATEGORY _____

Words _____   Words _____

_____   _____

_____   _____

_____   _____

_____   _____

58

CATEGORY _____

Words _____

_____

_____

_____

_____

CATEGORY _____

Words _____

_____

_____

_____

_____

CATEGORY _____

Words _____

_____

_____

_____

_____

CATEGORY _____

Words _____

_____

_____

_____

_____

CATEGORY _____

Words _____

_____

_____

_____

_____

CATEGORY _____

Words _____

_____

_____

_____

_____

CATEGORY _____

Words _____

_____

_____

_____

_____

CATEGORY _____

Words _____

_____

_____

_____

_____

UNIT V SUMMARY: PUTTING IDEAS TOGETHER

A category is a name for a group of ideas or pieces of information that have something in common.

For example, city, state, town and village all fit into the category of *units of government*.

When you organize ideas and information into categories, you can usually remember them better. Also you will discover how ideas and information are similar and how they are different.

59

110

ANSWERS FOR EXERCISES IN UNIT V

Page 45: Example

1. Los Angeles, New York, Toronto
2. Louisiana, Toronto, New Mexico, New Jersey ("ey" is considered a vowel combination, but you could also accept "y" as a consonant.)
3. Toronto
4. Answers will vary.

Pages 46-49: Exercise II

1. ocean, river, lake, stream, sea
2. ocean
3. Answers will vary.
4. Answers will vary.
5. hot, dry
6. cold, dark
7. hot, cold
8. Answers will vary.

9. empress
10. king
11. doctor, mechanic, pilot
12. Answers will vary.

13. plants, green
14. green
15. stems, plants
16. Answers will vary.

Pages 50-56: Exercise III

17. gasoline, wood, coal
18. gasoline, water
19. steel
20. Answers will vary.

Pages 50-56: Exercise III

21. heart, lung
22. fur, feather, skin, scales
23. none
24. Answers will vary.

25. computer, calculator
26. fraction, multiplication, subtraction, addition
27. multiplication, calculator
28. Answers will vary.

29. Accept reasonable answers.
30. Accept reasonable answers.
31. Accept reasonable answers.
32. Answers will vary.

33. b, c, f
34. a, d, e
35. d, e
36. Answers will vary.

37. all of them
38. d, e, f
39. a, d, e
40. Answers will vary.

41. b, d, g
42. c, e, f
43. a
44. Answers will vary.

45. a, c, e, g
46. b, d, f
47. all of them
48. Answers will vary.

Pages 57-59: Exercise IV

Answers will vary. Accept any answer that meets the definition of a category given on page 45.

ADDITIONAL SUGGESTIONS

1. Use categorization as a way to preview a new lesson or unit. For example, write LIVING THINGS on the board and say, "We are going to study a unit about living things today. Can you name some living things?" Your students will undoubtedly generate a long list of living things. Then you can discuss categories within the topic of *living things,* and have your class organize the items on the list into appropriate categories.

2. Collect many small items: a paper clip, nails, egg cartons, forks, spoons, spools of thread, needles and so on. Put students in small groups of 3-5 students. Have the students categorize the items in as many ways as possible. Ask them to name the categories into which these things fit. Have them "play around" with some of the concepts of categorization. For instance, if you have a category of *utensils found at home,* then *cooking utensils* and *sewing utensils* and *building utensils* equals the category of *utensils found at home.* And *utensils found at home* except for *building utensils* equals *cooking utensils* and *sewing utensils.* In other words, encourage your students to look at sets and subsets and the relationship between them.

3. Play games with your students that emphasize categorization whenever you have a few available minutes in class. Some examples are these:

   a. Set up a grid on the board like the one below. Have your students set up the same grid on a piece of scrap paper.

Categories

	Pets	Food	Famous People	Tools
F	fox terrier			
L				
B		bologna		
G				grinder
A			Anastasia	

   You may want to have your students suggest the categories and the letters of the alphabet in the grid.

   See how many unique items your students can suggest for each category. You may want to award points for each unique item.

   b. Play "Animal, Mineral, Vegetable" (also known as "Twenty Questions") with your students. Think of an animal, mineral, or object. Allow your students to ask twenty "yes" and "no" questions to try to guess the animal, mineral, or vegetable. They will need to use categorization to ask effective questions.

c. Send one student out of the room. Have the other students physically place themselves in categories, such as blond hair, over four feet tall, wearing shorts, with freckles, and so on. (You may want to guide the category choices and omit ones that may be sensitive.)

   Have the student return and guess why the other students are arranged as they are.

d. You supply the category name, and the students suggest items that belong to it. Try offering weird or humorous categories such as things that often cause allergies, or food that should not be eaten on the living room couch. Students may want to supply categories for their classmates.

e. Give your students a list of words with one word that doesn't belong, such as the following:

Winter Activities	Dangerous Animals	Wild Edibles
swim	bear	berries
ski	crocodile	corn
skate	kitten	fiddle heads
sled	lynx	butter nuts
sculpt snow	lion	mushrooms

   Have them name the category and fmd the word that doesn't belong. The students can make up similar lists and give them to each other.

4. Integrate the concept of categorization into whatever you are teaching. For example, if you are teaching a unit about plants, you could have your students collect a number of plants and examine the characteristics of plants. Then the students could arrange the plants by categories.

5. This may be an ideal time to start a computer data base with your students. Suggest a topic that you can add data to each day, such as weather or student lunch/attendance statistics. Have the students help you suggest the categories and log on the information daily.

6. Some software can give your students additional practice in categorization. You might want to review the *Inspiration CD-ROM* (Inspiration Software, 1999), which can also be downloaded from the WWW at www.inspiration.com.

7. Take out a number of books from your library from diverse categories: fiction, art, biography, sciences, travel, and so on. Cover the cataloguinbg number on each book, and have your students organize the books by category. You can do the same with any collection of artifacts: shells, coins, stamps, butterflies, minerals, and so on.

UNIT VI: PICTURING IN YOUR MIND'S EYE

In our culture we tend not to value the ability to visualize or think by imaging. One reason for this undervaluing is that when children begin to develop verbal and other symbolic skills, we encourage them to use these skills in place of their imaginative abilities rather than in conjunction with them.

Another reason is that the very nature of thinking in images or visualizing makes the process difficult to put into words and therefore problematic to define and incorporate within our educational structures. A third reason is that our world of media and print doesn't require the individual to rely upon her or his ability to image or "see with the mind's eye."

Research shows that the ability to visualize remains with most people through their early teens. Yet almost half of the adults in our society have lost that ability, probably largely from lack of use. The ability to imagine or see with the mind's eye can be a very powerful learning tool. This skill is associated in many cultures, including our own, with creativity, imagination, and intuition. Recently much research has been conducted with right and left brain functions and how these functions affect styles of learning. The research bears out what many teachers have known all along: that children learn well when they are encouraged to use their "right brain" ability to visualize. Through this ability they can learn to be active readers and listeners, to remember critical details, and to solve problems.

This unit is designed to (1) encourage and to validate the visualizing experience in your students, and to (2) provide some practical applications for imaging or visualization in your classroom.

Exercise I encourages your students to evoke their ability to picture in their mind's eye so that they can make use of this skill.

Exercise II puts this skill into the learning context of remembering critical details.

Exercises III and IV review some of the sequencing skills introduced in previous units. The student is encouraged to picture the steps needed to complete a task and to see how a whole learning task can be broken into achievable steps. These tasks also rely on the student's ability to think spatially as she or he pictures the process.

You'll want to try out Exercises III and IV yourself before you teach them, so you can gain experiential insight into how these activities work.

PLEASE NOTE: A small percentage of children in these grades may not be able to see visual imagery. Some of these children perceive their inner images not as pictures but as other kinds of sensation, for example, sounds, smells, and kinesthetic awareness. Still others, a very few, report no imagery at all.

YOUR STUDENTS WILL EACH NEED THREE SHEETS OF 8½" by 11" PAPER TO DO EXERCISE III. THEY WILL NEED RULERS TO COMPLETE EXERCISE IV.

115

UNIT VI: PICTURING IN YOUR MIND'S EYE

60

SUGGESTED DIRECTIONS FOR UNIT VI

PLEASE NOTE: This unit will require two 40 minute class periods.

DAY 1

1. Put your students in pairs, and have them open their **Student Texts** to pages 60-61. Then have a student read aloud the directions to the *Challenge* (page 61). Encourage your students to study the picture on page 60 and to pretend that they are in this city.

   Approximate time: 5 minutes

116

CHALLENGE

Directions: Study the picture on page 60. Imagine yourself in this part of this city. Your teacher will give you some suggestions for imagining. Listen to them first. Then try the four challenges below.

1. Imagine that you are at Point A, at the top of the building looking down at the city below. Describe what you see to your partner.

2. Now in your mind's eye, go across the street to Point B. Tell your partner how the city looks from this viewpoint. What things are different? What things are the same?

3. Now you are down the street at Point C. Imagine what the city looks like from here. Describe what you see to your partner.

4. Try imagining that you are sitting in a car at Point D. Look out the window, and tell your partner how you see things differently.

61

2. Give your students the following suggestions before they begin the *Challenge:*

"Sometimes closing your eyes and being very quiet helps you to see in your mind's eye. You may want to look at the picture again and then be very quiet as you try to do the challenge.

"Some of you may not actually see pictures. But you will have a sense of things, such as how the truck will look as seen from above or how the buildings will seem high when you are down in the city. Try to make use of your way of sensing things.

"Some of you will observe other things about the city such as the smell of the exhaust, the sounds of traffic, or the feel of the air on a breezy perch. Since these sensations can be very interesting, try to take note of them as well as what you are 'seeing' in your mind's eye."

Have the students read the four challenges to themselves, read them aloud to your students, or have a student or students read them aloud. Then ask your students to do the four challenges. Give them time to do so.

After a few minutes, ask the students to share their experience of doing the four challenges with their partners. Give your students a few minutes to discuss their experience. Then engage the whole class in discussion. In particular invite students to share what kinds of imagery they experienced.

15-18 minutes

3. Read the *Introduction* (page 62) aloud, or have a student read it aloud. Discuss briefly.

5 minutes

4. Read the directions to Exercise I with your students. Then read the story below aloud. The story also appears in the **Student Text,** so students can refer to it after they finish the questions on pages 63-64. While you read the story, do not have your students look at the text.

The city's skyline seemed to reach down and choke Mindy. She looked for something familiar, but all she saw was a blur of faces and the drab color of winter clothes as a rush of human bodies pushed her aside. She would have liked to have gone into the coffee shop. She was standing right in front of it. It looked so inviting with its neatly set tables and windows full of plants. But if she went in, she might not see her father who was supposed to be here at two o'clock.

"Are you lost, little girl?"

Mindy looked up alarmed. The face peering at her was not an unkind one. The woman had too much make-up on. But her rounded cheeks, plump body, and even her hair pulled up into a tight bun reminded Mindy of her art teacher who was a kind woman. However, Mindy was horrified af at the thought of telling her story to a stranger.

"No, ma'am. Thank you m'am. I'm quite all right." The woman continued to peer into Mindy's face. It was obvious that she didn't want to leave the frail girl alone. Mindy saw the look of concern and flashed the woman a smile that she hoped looked confident.

"My dad will be right here."

"Well, child, if he doesn't come, look me up. I work at Mademoiselle's." The woman pointed her gloved hand to a large purple building with green and pink awnings across the street and down the block. "My name is Harriet, and I can stop work any time to help a young friend."

"Thank you, Ma'am. But my father will be here. I just got here too early." Mindy hoped she sounded more confident than she felt.

Harriet walked away briskly, turning every so often to send a worried smile back at Mindy. Mindy tried to look perky. She remembered her grandmother saying, "Look perky, child. You wear your troubles on your sleeve — an open book for all the world to see." She tried not to look lost and hopeless, which was how she felt. She desperately hoped no one else would ask her what she was doing on this corner.

The fact was that Mindy wasn't early. No matter how much her adored father tried, he could never get to a place on time. Knowing her father, she had planned to be at this meeting place exactly on time. She knew he would be late, so she didn't want to be early. She also didn't want to be late and give him time to wander off window shopping in one of his daydreams. She had climbed into the taxi, given the man the address, and landed on the corner of Elm and Vine exactly at two o'clock.

The old church across from where Mindy stood had probably once seemed huge to the bypasser. Now it was dwarfed by the larger buildings around it. Still, it was an impressive place. The paved paths through its neat gardens, the lovely fountain, and the solid steps leading up to the great double wooden doors gave the church a look of commanding calm. It looked like a place where a person could go and be soothed. Mindy wished she could go now and sit by the fountain, but if she did that, her father surely would never find her. She looked at the large clock on the church tower.

Two thirty! Even her absent minded father wouldn't have her stay in an unknown spot of this busy city for a half hour all by herself. She shivered in the coat she had chosen to wear. Her prettier coat wasn't nearly as warm as the dull practical one that she had left hanging in the closet. The thin, lacy dress beneath it wasn't much help either. She was starting to get cold, really cold, and scared. She stopped caring if she wore her emotions on her sleeve. She was scared, cold, alone, and angry with her father who had deserted her in this place filled with a thousand strangers.

"Listen, honey," a voice broke into her angry thoughts. She jumped and turned nervously to the loud voice. It was Harriet again. "I've been watching you from the shop. I don't understand what a little girl would be doing standing all alone on a street corner in this city. Come on in here. You can have a hot chocolate and tell me about it."

Mindy was about to refuse, but she couldn't think of any good reason to give. She let herself be led into the warm coffee shop.

"Where do you think you are going with my little girl?" boomed a deep voice behind them. Mindy was flooded with relief. Her father had come after all! She quickly untangled her hand from Harriet's gloved fingers and jumped into her father's open arms.

INTRODUCTION

The first two units in this *Program* asked you to picture things in your mind's eye. You are probably better at this than you realize. If you could picture or imagine any details about the picture of page 60, then you already picture things in your mind quite well. If that task was difficult for you, you have probably imagined a solution to a problem such as how to build a model, sew pieces together to make clothes, or take a short cut through the neighborhood. Also you can probably close your eyes right now and, in your mind's eye, see your teacher's face. Doing any of these tasks shows that you are able to imagine or picture things in your mind's eye.

You may not have thought that this ability to picture or imagine could help you with your school work. However, picturing is an important study skill. Picturing in your mind's eye can help you be an active listener, remember details, and solve problems. In this unit you will learn about some of the ways that picturing can help you.

PICTURES IN YOUR MIND: ACTIVE LISTENING

EXERCISE I

Directions: Your teacher is going to read a short story to you. As your teacher reads the story, try to imagine or picture details in your mind. After the story is finished, you will be asked to answer some questions about what things in the story look like.

***NOTE: While you're listening, try to get comfortable, so that you can really picture the details. If it helps, you can close your eyes.

Have the students write their responses to the questions on pages 63-64 without looking at their copies of the story. When they have done so, discuss the responses as a class. Then note that a copy of the story is in the **Student Text** if students want to read it over.

1. Was the sun shining? _____

2. What does Mindy look like? What color hair does she have? How tall is she? What color eyes does she have?

   _____

   _____

   _____

   _____

3. What color hair does Harriet have? What is she wearing? _____

   _____

4. Did you picture buildings other than the coffee shop, the church, and Mademoiselle's? What did they look like? Were the buildings shops? Offices? Restaurants?

   _____

   _____

   _____

5. What kind of a shop is Mademoiselle's? _____

   _____

6. Can you imagine the coat Mindy has on? What color is it? What material is it made from?

   _____

   _____

   _____

7. Can you imagine the dress Mindy has on? What color is it? Does it have long sleeves or short sleeves?

   _____

   _____

   _____

Continued on page 64.

63

8. Describe the church across the street. How big is it? What material is it made from? Does it have any windows?

_____

_____

_____

_____

9. Does the street have any traffic? _____

_____

10. What does Mindy's father look like? _____

_____

_____

64

122

The city's skyline seemed to reach down and choke Mindy. She looked for something familiar, but all she saw was a blur of faces and the drab color of winter clothes as a rush of human bodies pushed her aside. She would have liked to have gone into the coffee shop. She was standing right in front of it. It looked so inviting with its neatly set tables and windows full of plants. But if she went in, she might not see her father who was supposed to be here at two o'clock.

"Are you lost, little girl?"

Mindy looked up alarmed. The face peering at her was not an unkind one. The woman had too much make-up on. But her rounded cheeks, plump body, and even her hair pulled up into a tight bun reminded Mindy of her art teacher who was a kind woman. However, Mindy was horrified at the thought of telling her story to a stranger.

"No, ma'am. Thank you m'am. I'm quite all right." The woman continued to peer into Mindy's face. It was obvious that she didn't want to leave the frail girl alone. Mindy saw the look of concern and flashed the woman a smile that she hoped looked confident.

"My dad will be right here."

"Well, child, if he doesn't come, look me up. I work at Mademoiselle's." The woman pointed her gloved hand to a large purple building with green and pink awnings across the street and down the block. "My name is Harriet, and I can stop work any time to help a young friend."

"Thank you, Ma'am. But my father will be here. I just got here too early." Mindy hoped she sounded more confident than she felt.

Harriet walked away briskly, turning every so often to send a worried smile back at Mindy. Mindy tried to look perky. She remembered her grandmother saying, "Look perky, child. You wear your troubles on your sleeve — an open book for all the world to see." She tried not to look lost and hopeless, which was how she felt. She desperately hoped no one else would ask her what she was doing on this corner.

The fact was that Mindy wasn't early. No matter how much her adored father tried, he could never get to a place on time. Knowing her father, she had planned to be at this meeting place exactly on time. She knew he would be late, so she didn't want to be early. She also didn't want to be late and give him time to wander off window shopping in one of his daydreams. She had climbed into the taxi, given the man the address, and landed on the corner of Elm and Vine exactly at two o'clock.

The old church across from where Mindy stood had probably once seemed huge to the bypasser. Now it was dwarfed by the larger buildings around it. Still, it was an impressive place. The paved paths through its neat gardens, the lovely fountain, and the solid steps leading up to the great double wooden doors gave the church a look of commanding calm. It looked like a place where a person could go and be soothed. Mindy wished she could go now and sit by the fountain, but if she did that, her father surely would never find her. She looked at the large clock on the church tower.

Continued on page 66.

65

123

Two thirty! Even her absent minded father wouldn't have her stay in an unknown spot of this busy city for a half hour all by herself. She shivered in the coat she had chosen to wear. Her prettier coat wasn't nearly as warm as the dull practical one that she had left hanging in the closet. The thin, lacy dress beneath it wasn't much help either. She was starting to get cold, really cold, and scared. She stopped caring if she wore her emotions on her sleeve. She was scared, cold, alone, and angry with her father who had deserted her in this place filled with a thousand strangers.

"Listen, honey," a voice broke into her angry thoughts. She jumped and turned nervously to the loud voice. It was Harriet again. "I've been watching you from the shop. I don't understand what a little girl would be doing standing all alone on a street corner in this city. Come on in here. You can have a hot chocolate and tell me about it."

Mindy was about to refuse, but she couldn't think of any good reason to give. She let herself be led into the warm coffee shop.

"Where do you think you are going with my little girl?" boomed a deep voice behind them. Mindy was flooded with relief. Her father had come after all! She quickly untangled her hand from Harriet's gloved fingers and jumped into her father's open arms.

66

124

MAKING THE PICTURES WORK FOR YOU: REMEMBERING DETAILS

When you answered the questions about Mindy's story, you were probably using pictures in your mind or imagery. Imagining characters and scenes helps to make a story interesting. None of the answers were really in the story! You made them up in your mind's eye, that is, your imagination. When you get a picture of characters or scenery from reading or listening to a story, it shows that you have a creative imagination.

You can use this ability to *see in your mind's eye* to help you make sense of some details that may not be clear to you.

When you do the next exercise, you can put this imagination to work for you.

EXERCISE II

Directions: Your teacher will read a selection aloud called "The Body's Defense Against Disease." As you listen, try to picture the following things:

1. The first line of defense is described as an obstacle course. Try to picture the obstacles that get in the way of germs.

2. Part of the second line of defense is the white blood cells. Try to picture what the white blood cells look like as they surround a germ.

3. The third line of defense is antibodies. When you hear about antibodies, try to form a picture of them.

4. As you hear about the following things, try to get a picture of each one in your mind's eye: germs, lymph, capillaries, and infection.

When the reading is completed, you will be asked to answer some factual questions.

Again, it might help you to close your eyes, so you can picture things without interference as you listen.

67

5. Read *Making The Picture Work For You: Remember the Details* (page 67) aloud, or have a student or students read it aloud. Discuss briefly. Then read the directions for Exercise II with your students. Discuss for clarity and emphasis. Then read aloud the selection on the next page to your students.

THE BODY'S DEFENSE AGAINST DISEASE

Since germs are present everywhere, you might think it amazing that we are not ill all the time. The reason we aren't is that the human body is armed to defend itself against infection and disease. The body has three lines of defense.

The first line of defense in the body is an obstacle course for germs. There are certain parts of your body that actually block germs from entering your blood stream. These body parts are the skin, mucous in your nose and mouth, and stomach acids. The skin makes a thin but tough barrier for germs. When germs try to enter through the nose and mouth, thick mucous often blocks them. (That's the reason for your runny nose when you have a cold.) A final obstacle for the germs is stomach acids. It's difficult for the germs to get past these acids, which dissolve them in seconds.

If a germ should enter your bloodstream, however, you have an even more impressive force ready to do battle with the foreign invader. This is your second line of defense. An army of tiny white blood cells is always on the lookout for disease. The white blood cells themselves are so small that they squeeze through the walls of capillaries — the tinest of blood vessels — to find the disease-causing germ. The white blood cells swarm around any foreign object such as a germ and devour it before it can do any harm to your body. Then a clear liquid in your blood called lymph washes away the digested germs and left over white blood cells. During this struggle to free itself from germs, your body often gets overheated. The fever you develop wipes out the germs that need to live in low temperatures. Your body is now freed from the chance of infection.

Sometimes a germ does manage to get through the first two lines of defense. When this happens, your body's secret service springs into action. Your secret service is made up of antibodies that hide out in the blood cells until they need to be called into the fight. Each secret service agent or antibody is trained to fight off a certain germ. If that special germ gets through the first two lines of defense, the antibody charges out of hiding and surrounds and disintegrates the germ.

Of course, germs do sneak by and manage to make us sick at times. But our body's three lines of defense keep us pretty healthy when you consider the ever present germ!

Have your students write the answers to the questions and do the *For Fun* (page 68). Discuss the answers to these questions. Ask your students how imaging helped them answer the questions.

12-15 minutes

126

ANSWER THESE QUESTIONS

1. Name two things that provide an obstacle course in the body's first line of defense.

   _____

   _____

2. How do white blood cells help the body protect you from germs? _____

   _____

   _____

3. What is a capillary? _____

4. What does an antibody do to protect you from germs? _____

   _____

   _____

5. How does lymph help your body to handle germs? _____

   _____

   _____

FOR FUN

1. Draw a germ as you pictured it.

68

2. Did any other interesting visual images come into your mind as you listened? If so, draw or explain them in words.

KINDS OF PICTURES IN YOUR MIND'S EYE

When people imagine, they often see pictures or images in their mind's eye. Sometimes the imagination includes other senses as well: hearing, smelling, touching, even tasting. In fact, when some people imagine, they don't see pictures at all. Instead they hear, smell, touch, taste, or all of these.

Everyone can imagine, but we all use our imagination in our own personal way. What do you experience when *you* imagine?

69

6. Read aloud *Kinds of Pictures in Your Mind's Eye* (page 69). Discuss briefly.

3-5 minutes

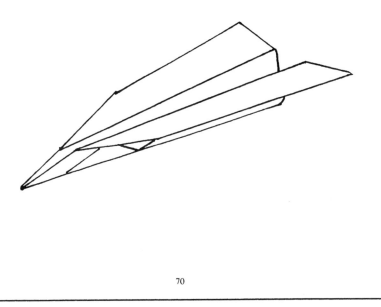
DAY 2

1. Read *Solve Your Problem By Picturing The Steps* (page 70) aloud with your students.

    Hand our three blank 8½″ by 11″ sheets of paper to each student. Read the directions for Exercise III (page 70) aloud. Organize your students into pairs or small groups for this exercise. Explain that while you want the members of each pair or group to work together, each student should make her or his own airplane. When your students understand the instructions, have them begin the activity. As they work, circulate among them and give encouragement and help as needed. When your students have completed Method 3, give them a minute to fly their airplanes. Then engage them in discussing the three methods and how they used imagery.

METHOD II

Read the step-by-step instructions below. Follow each of the steps. Try to construct the paper airplane they describe.

STEP 1

Use a sheet of 8½" x 11" paper. Crease-fold the paper in half first. Then open it. Fold the top corners down.

STEP 2

Hold the paper lengthwise. Call the top left point A and the bottom left point B. Fold A and B down about a quarter of the sides to the crease. Make sure A and B touch on the center crease.

STEP 3

Call the top points of the airplane's nose C and D. Fold in points C and D. The top two edges should meet each other on the center crease.

STEP 4

Fold the entire airplane in half in the opposite direction.

STEP 5

Fold the wings down to meet the bottom edge of the fuselage.

STEP 6

Curl the tail section up slightly for better lift.

71

130

Look at the pictures in the steps below. The pictures show what the airplane should look like *as* you follow the directions for each step. Try to match what you are doing to what you see.

STEP 1

Use a sheet of 8½″ x 11″ paper. Crease-fold the paper in half first. Then open it. Fold the top corners down.

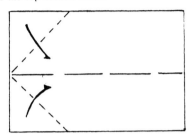

STEP 2

Fold in the sides. Make sure that points A and B touch each other on the center crease.

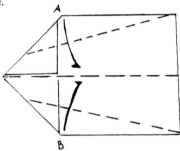

STEP 3

Fold in points C and D. The top two edges should meet each other on the center crease.

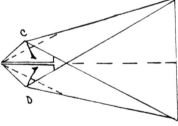

72

131

STEP 4

Fold the entire airplane in half in the opposite direction.

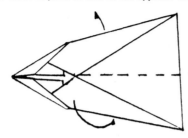

STEP 5

Fold the wings down to meet the bottom edge of the fuselage.

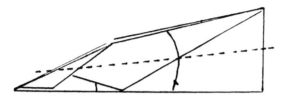

STEP 6

Curl the tail section up slightly for better lift.

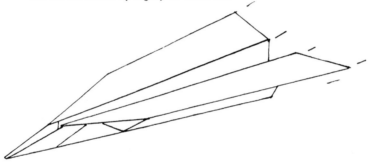

2. Read the directions to Exercise IV (page 74) aloud, or have a student or students read them aloud. Discuss ways to solve the problem together. If the students seem frustrated, suggest making a grid over each square as below. Such a grid will allow the students to deal with one small piece of the larger map at a time.

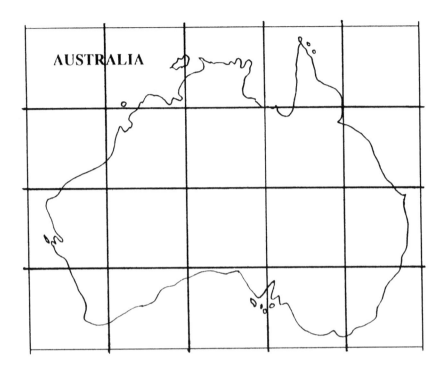

If time allows, have your students do Exercise IV now, using the grid method or another approach of their choosing. When they are done, have them share their drawings and discuss them in small groups. If time is short, have your students complete Exercise IV for homework. Then have the small group discussions the next day.

15-20 minutes

EXERCISE IV

Directions: Look at the map below. You have to copy this map in the space below it as accurately as possible. Can you think of a way to break this task into steps? Discuss this problem with your classmates and teacher before you begin.

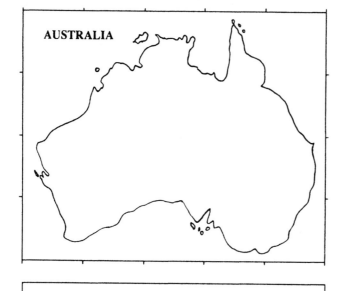

74

UNIT VI SUMMARY: PICTURING IN YOUR MIND'S EYE

Most people have the ability to imagine or see pictures in their mind's eye. Sometimes the imagination uses your other senses: hearing, smelling, feeling, even tasting.

These pictures or images can help to make reading and hearing stories more interesting to you. You can also remember important details when you form images of them.

The ability to picture things in your mind's eye is often helpful in solving problems. When you use your imagination to help you solve a problem, break the problem down into small, easy-to-do steps. Then do one step at a time.

75

3. Read aloud the *Summary* (page 75) with your students. Discuss for clarity and emphasis.

   3-5 minutes

ANSWERS FOR EXERCISES IN UNIT VI

Pages 63-64: Exercise I

Answers will vary.

Page 68: Exercise II

1. skin, mucous in your nose and mouth, stomach acids
2. White blood cells surround a germ and disintegrate it.
3. the smallest of the blood vessels
4. Antibodies are in the blood cells and are designed to fight off certain germs.
5. Lymph is a clear liquid that washes away the waste after germs have been disintegrated.

FOR FUN

Answers will vary.

ADDITIONAL SUGGESTIONS

1. Give your students diagrams of models (birdhouses, dollhouses, planes, cars, and so on). Ask them to study the diagrams and try to picture in their mind's eye what the completed model would look like. Then have your students describe what they imagine.

2. Prepare two lists: one of abstract things; the other of things that have high visual content. Two examples are listed below. Give the students the abstract list first. Tell them to try to memorize the list in one minute. Then wait for a minute, and have the students write down as many words as they can remember from the list. Repeat this procedure with the visual list.

   Research shows that people picture the visual list in their mind's eye as they are trying to memorize the words and consequently remember that list with greater accuracy. Your students' experience is likely to bear out this finding. Discuss what happened as your students were trying to memorize each list. Point out that seeing things in their mind's eye helps them to retain information.

ABSTRACT LIST	VISUAL LIST
term	sunset
height	umbrella
fill	red
send	tiger
theory	window
loss	glow
ask	diamond
certain	daisy
said	chair
element	moon

136

3. Give your students a problem that forces them to visualize the building they are in. For example, tell them to imagine that they have been left alone in the building. All the windows and doors are locked with the exception of one. Be specific about the one window or door that is unlocked, and make this exit as far away and indirect as possible. Ask the students to imagine the fastest way to get out of the building using this exit.

4. Put your students in pairs. Tell them that they will be giving each other oral directions on how to get somewhere, but they won't know where their partner is taking them until the end of the directions. They must not draw diagrams or take notes. (Make sure the places you choose will be well known by all your students.) Give each student a piece of paper with a destination written on it. Have your students give each other directions *without* telling the partner the destination. The direction-giver is successful if his or her partner ends up knowing what his or her destination is.

   This game requires both the direction-giver and the direction-follower to use visual clues to construct a mental map.

5. Ask your students to imagine the room they are sitting in from a different angle. For example, have the student in the first row imagine that she or he is in the last seat in the back row. See if he or she can picture the room from this new angle. Then have him or her go to the new place and see how accurate his or her imagination was.

   This kind of exercise is a good introduction to a creative writing assignment that requires a first person character to describe different settings.

6. A good source for understanding the right side of the brain and its impact on educational issues is *Drawing On The Right Side of The Brain* by Betty Edwards (Los Angeles: J.P. Tarcher, 1979). Although this book describes a course in visual art, its applications can have impact on many areas of an academic curriculum.

7. Have your students make mental maps of their neighborhood or town. You can do this by asking them to close their eyes and imagine a walk from one point to another. Tell them to pay particular attention to anything they can sense (smell, touch, see, hear, taste) along the way. Give them at least five minutes to do this task. Then have your students draw a diagram of what they imagined. Have your students compare their diagrams. You will find that they have highly personalized mental maps. A good resource for understanding this is *The Mind's Eye* by Robert Sommer (New York: Dell, 1978).

8. When you want your students to memorize certain facts, play around with the idea of storing these facts in mental images. For instance, say you wanted them to memorize the names of the great lakes. Have them take the first initial from each lake and make up a phrase describing something they could imagine: Susan and Mary Hike Ever Onward.

9. Give your students verbal tasks that are difficult to do, such as describing a spiral staircase, telling someone how to tie a shoe, explaining to someone how to focus a microscope, and so on. Invite them to develop creative ways to do these tasks.

10. Ask your students to imagine doing a physical task before they actually enact it. For example, you might ask a student to imagine he or she is about to pitch a ball. Ask him or her to imagine his or her body as it goes through each stage of the process of pitching. Then have him or her pitch a ball. Question him or her to see if he or she could use his or her imaging in the process of pitching.

11. Although television has been cited as one cause of the demise of our visual skills, it can also be used to enhance the experience of inner imagery. Some of the ways this can be done are described below:

    a. View a documentary on a certain country or place to which most of your students have never traveled. Then discuss that setting in terms of categories beyond what the television can show. Talk about the aromas, the feel, the flavors, and the different scenes of the new place. Ask your students to imagine that they are visiting this place and to write a diary entry about a day in this place.

    b. Read a novel that has been dramatized. Before you watch the video dramatization, have your students discuss their image of the characters and settings. Then have your students watch the dramatization. Critique the portrayal of character and setting by having the students compare the video images with the images they had previously formed.

    c. Describe a scientific process, such as the division of cells. As you do so, encourage your students to imagine this process. Then show a video depicting the process. Have the students compare their inner image to the video. Do this repeatedly with different processes to encourage the students' ability to visualize.

    d. Get your students to critique certain advertisements by discussing the power of visual imagery. Discuss the product as it is presented on the sceen, and compare it to the actual product. Discuss how visual media encourages people to buy things they may not want or need.

12. The problems presented in this unit are concrete, spatial problems. However, visualization can also help on abstract levels. An example of this is when Archimedes climbed into the bath tub and shouted "Eureka" because he was finally able to imagine how the problem of weighing the king's gold could be solved. His own body's displacment of the water gave him the image he needed to solve the problem. Children also experience this "Ah Ha" phenomenon.

   Explaining abstract scientific problems in a visual way often encourages children to use their intuition and ability to imagine. There are many scientific problems that lend themselves to a visual description. How does a prism break up white light into colors? How can certain weather conditions cause people to see mirages? How are a bee's eyes structured to highlight the flowers with the greatest honey producing capacity? Science can provide a wonderful context for inviting children to think both visually and intuitively.

13. After your students have read a novel, ask them to become "movie producers." Ask them to think about where and how they would stage the story and what kinds of props, backdrops, and weather conditions they would need. Also ask them to imagine what actresses or actors would be the most appropriate for the main characters.

UNIT VII: READING FOR MEANING

This unit and the two that follow it compose a sequence that focuses on reading a textbook, taking notes from reading, and taking notes from listening. As the foundation skills involved in these tasks are much the same, these units can be seen as parts of a whole. You may want to examine all three of these units before you begin to teach Unit VII.

When faced with a reading assignment in a text, most students in the middle school years begin with the first word in the assignment and continue as far as their interest, sense of duty, or fear of failure carries them. Yet regardless of how far they get in their reading, the method used is the same ineffective one because the reading is done without thought or purpose.

This unit introduces your students to a way of reading texts that can be much more effective for learning than starting with the first word and reading as far as one gets. The method is *reading for meaning,* and it includes four steps: Surveying, Reading, Mapping, and Checking yourself.

Integrated with the *reading for meaning* method are several important concepts and skills. Your students are probably familiar with some of these and unfamiliar with others. While these skills and concepts can be taught separately, we have presented them in an integrated way in this unit because this is the way a student would actually use them.

The skills and concepts are the following:

1. *Understanding what main ideas and supporting details are and locating them in a paragraph or passage*

   This is a key thinking skill with which your students may need additional work. Several useful sources for teaching main ideas and supporting details are listed in the *Additional Suggestions* in this unit.

2. *Recognizing the topic sentence of a paragraph*

   Some of your students will probably be familiar with this skill but may need review. Others may require more specific instruction. Also, you may want to give all of your students practice in locating topic sentences in the beginning, middle, and end of paragraphs. You may also want to examine paragraphs that don't state the topic sentence at all. A good way to have the students review this skill further is to have them write sample paragraphs.

3. *Surveying*

   Your students may already know about a related skill called *scanning. You* can introduce them to *surveying* by comparing it with *scanning.* Another introductory exercise that you may want to use is this: hand your students various paperback books and ask them, "Which of these books do you think you'd like to read?" They'll probably 'survey' the books by checking the titles, number of pages, size of print, kinds of illustrations, and so on. Perhaps they will read a little of the texts. When your students have finished "surveying," discuss with them what they have done to examine the books and what they have learned from this.

4. *Mapping*

   Mapping is a pictorial method of taking notes. As students of middle school age are highly tactually and visually oriented, they can often work with ideas more effectively through pictorial or visual representations. Such representations also help them to retain the ideas. Outlining, the traditional method for taking notes, is introduced in the following unit.

Mapping is an alternative method that can prove extremely useful to students for whom pictorial representations of ideas and information are easier to create, manipulate, and recall than linear representations, such as outlining. Mapping is also very useful in situations where the presentation lacks a clear sense of organization, such as class discussions.

If mapping is new to you, we suggest that you examine it carefully, experiment with its applications, and help your students master its uses if you share our perception of its value. If you are interested in learning more about mapping, we suggest that you examine *Designs for Self-Instruction* by Johanna Keirns (Allyn & Bacon, 1999) or *Great Teaching with Graphic Organizers* by Patti Drapeau (Scholastic Inc., 1998).

5. *Checking yourself*

When students first try this step, they often gain more by telling what they know to each other, or, when possible, to an older student or an adult. As they speak, they often discover the gaps in their understanding of what they have read. As students become more confident about this step, they are more likely to use selfrecitation effectively.

You may want to give your students practice with this step by having them "check themselves" with peers. You might also encourage them to use this step by talking with their parents and older siblings.

We offer two alternatives for teaching this unit. You will want to read through alternatives carefully to choose the one best suited for your class.

The first alternative is best suited to a group of students who have already had some exposure to "reading for meaning." In this alternative, we suggest that you take several days to introduce the concepts separately. Then you will want to put them all together by teaching the "reading for meaning" method, using the content from your own curriculum.

A NOTE ABOUT TEACHING METHODS

The usefulness to any student of the "reading for meaning" method clearly depends on his or her ability to use the method individually. For the purpose of introducing students to this method, we strongly recommend that you organize your class into small goups, as noted in the Directions below. Many students will find the "reading for meaning" method detailed and challenging. Students working in groups will be more willing to become engaged in learning the various steps of the method as a result of their participation in a group. Encourage your students to share the work of the group actively, even if it seems inefficient at times. Then, after the initial lesson, you can structure assignments that will require the student to use the "reading for meaning" method on an individual basis.

UNIT VII: READING FOR MEANING

HOW DO YOU READ?

*"Read the assignment in your book,
and be ready for a quiz!"*

This is a direction you probably often hear in school. When you are given this direction, what do you do?

Look at the reading on page 77 of this unit. If your teacher asked you to read this and be ready for a quiz about it, what would you do? On the lines below, briefly describe *how* you would complete this assignment.

REMEMBER: Don't actually read the section now. Just describe *how* you would read it.

_____

_____

_____

_____

_____

_____

76

SUGGESTED DIRECTIONS FOR UNIT VII

First Alternative

DAY 1

1. At the beginning of the period, divide your class into small groups of two or three members. Have your students work all of the exercises in these groups, with the exception of *How Do You Read?* Have them do *How Do You Read?* individually.

2. Read *How Do You Read?* (page 76) aloud to your students. If necessary, briefly clarify the assignment. Then tell your students that they will have two minutes to complete the assignment. When they are done, have several students read aloud what they have written. See if other students have different responses. Discuss briefly. Then read the *Introduction* (page 78) aloud to your students, or have a student read it aloud.

Approximate time: 5-10 minutes

THE RACE TO THE MOON

Sputnik launched!

On October 4, 1957, the U.S.S.R. astounded the American public by launching Sputnik I. Sputnik I was the first man-made satellite to orbit the earth. On November 3rd of the same year, the Soviets sent another Sputnik, Sputnik II, into orbit, carrying a dog named Laika. The race to the moon was on.

The United States responds.

The United States was caught off guard by the advanced technology of the Soviet space program. In the year following the launching of Sputnik I, the United States Congress authorized billions of dollars to be put into an American space program. NASA, the National Aeronautics and Space Administration, was created in 1958. In that same year the United States launched its first satellite, Explorer I.

The first travelers in space

A few years later the Soviet Union sent the first traveler into outer space. On April 7, 1961, Yuri Gagarin became the first man to journey into the farthest reaches of the Earth's atmosphere. In 1963 Valentina Tereshkova became the first woman to fly into outer space.

The first American astronaut

In the years between 1961 and 1963 the American space program was also busy. The United States launched its first manned flight in May 1961. Alan Shepherd rode a tiny capsule which was launched from Cape Canaveral in Florida. Shepherd's flight lasted only fifteen minutes. Americans huddled around their TV sets to watch the launch. Telstar, the first communications satellite, was also launched in 1961.

Amazing breakthroughs in 1965

Amazing breakthroughs engineered by both countries took place in 1965. Leonov of the U.S.S.R. made the first space walk from the Voshkod spacecraft. The United States launched the first of the Gemini space flights, each of which orbited the Earth many times. Luna 9 of the U.S.S.R. and Surveyor I of the U.S.A. were both unmanned spacecrafts which made soft landings on the moon during this year. A Soviet probe crash-landed on Venus. And the U.S.'s Mariner 4 transmitted the first close-up pictures of Mars over a distance of 217 million kilometers.

Orbiting the moon

After many different kinds of space experiments had been conducted by both nations, the United States made a great thrust to the moon in 1968. The American astronauts Frank Borman, William Anders, and James Lovell, Jr. orbited the moon ten times on December 24-25 of that year.

Moon landing!

Finally in July 1969 American astronauts Armstrong and Aldrin placed their feet on the surface of the moon. The race between nations was over. The plaque the astronauts left on the moon said: "Here men from Earth first set forth on the moon. July 1969 A.D. We came in peace for all mankind."

77

145

INTRODUCTION

You've probably discovered that many students don't have a special way of reading a textbook. What they usually do is start with the first word in the assignment and read as far as they get. Unfortunately this isn't a very good way to learn from your reading.

This unit will show you a way of reading an assignment in a textbook and learning from your reading. This method is called READING FOR MEANING. You may find that this method is new to you and will take a little more time at first. You might also find it a little tricky. Stay with it! Learn how to use this method, and you will become a better learner.

READING FOR MEANING

When you read a paragraph or section in your textbook, what you really want to find out is:

What is the *main idea* of this reading?

What are the *important details* that support the *main idea?*

READING FOR MEANING means locating *main ideas* and the *supporting details* in your reading.

Another way to think of READING FOR MEANING is this: when you read for meaning, you're trying to find out what the paragraph or section is trying to tell you. Ask yourself these questions:

What does the person who wrote this paragraph or section want me to know?

What is this paragraph or section trying to tell me?

3. Read aloud *Reading For Meaning* (page 78), or have a student read it aloud. Discuss briefly for emphasis. Then have your students do Exercise I (page 79). Go over the exercise.

5-10 minutes

EXERCISE 1

Directions: Read the paragraph below. Then write the main idea of the paragraph on the lines that follow.

REMEMBER: The *main idea* in a paragraph is the most important idea. It is the idea that the rest of the paragraph is about.

The *main idea* is the idea that the writer is trying to share with you.

PARAGRAPH A

Dogs have a very powerful sense of smell that they can use to find things. Police use tracking dogs to search for people who are missing in the woods. The dogs sniff a piece of clothing owned by the missing person. Then they try to track the scent in the area where the person was last seen. Often these dogs can find people who are lost when the police have no other way of locating them. Another kind of tracking dog is the hunting hound. These dogs can follow animals for miles through the forest once they have sniffed their scent. Though some dogs are better than others in using their sense of smell, all dogs have a stronger sense of smell than people do.

_____

_____

79

147

MAIN IDEA AND SUPPORTING DETAILS

We know that the *main idea* of a paragraph is the most important idea in that paragraph. It's the idea that the rest of the paragraph is about.

Most paragraphs also have *supporting details.* Supporting details explain, prove, or tell something about the main idea of the paragraph. They make the main idea more clear to us or give us more information about it.

These details are called *"supporting"* details because they *"hold up"* the main idea. This means that they give us reasons to believe the main idea and help us to understand it.

EXERCISE II

Directions: Read the paragraph on page 79 again. On the lines below, list *two* supporting details for the main idea.

PARAGRAPH A

1. _____

2. _____

4. Have a student read aloud *Main Idea And Supporting Details* (page 80), or read it aloud yourself. Have your students do Exercise II (page 80). Go over the exercise.

    5-10 minutes

5. Omit Exercise III.

EXERCISE III

Directions: Find the main idea for the paragraph below. Then locate two supporting details. Write the main idea and supporting details on the appropriate lines. Do the same for Paragraphs C and D on page 82.

PARAGRAPH B

In the early days America was a country full of individuals who did many things well. One man stands out from all the rest. This man helped to organize many institutions in the new country: the United States Post Office; the Pennsylvania Academy; Pennsylvania Hospital, the first in America. He also organized the first American expedition to the Arctic region. He was an inventor, inventing many useful things including the Franklin stove, the lightning rod, bifocal glasses, and an instrument he call the "armonica." He also wrote books and newspapers and took part in the politics of early America. Benjamin Franklin was a man of many talents.

Main Idea: _____

_____

Supporting details:

1. _____

2. _____

81

149

PARAGRAPH C

She was an adult female who died three million years ago. The archaeologists who found her bones nicknamed her "Lucy." They did not find her entire skeleton. However, a description of Lucy can be based on the bones they found. She was a Hominidae, a primate that stood and walked on two legs. She had a skeleton much like ours. But she was tiny compared to today's humans. She stood three feet, eight inches tall and weighed about 65 pounds. Her thick bones show that she must have had great muscular strength. Lucy's face and apelike jutting jaws were large, but her brain was probably only one third the size of a modern human's.

Main Idea: _____

_____

Supporting details:

1. _____

2. _____

PARAGRAPH D

The man lowered a hydrophone into the water. This phone was meant to pick up the clicks, whistles, and short piercing screams of the killer whales. He explained that the clicks seem to be a way that the whales tell each other where food is located. The whistles are heard most often between resting or socializing whales. But, he explained, the most interesting of all are the screams. They are different within each whale pod (a pod is a group of whales). This suggests that whales are among the few animals that have a local dialect or a special way of speaking to the others that live in the same region.

Main Idea: _____

_____

Supporting details:

1. _____

2. _____

82

150

HOW DO YOU FIND THE MAIN IDEA?

The main idea of a paragraph is stated in the *topic sentence*. The purpose of the *topic sentence* is to tell you the main idea. For example, in the paragraph about the strong sense of smell that dogs have, the topic sentence is the first one.

When you read a paragraph, the main idea will sometimes be very clear to you. When it's not clear, use these hints for finding it:

1. Most often the topic sentence is the first sentence in the paragraph. This means that you'll often find the main idea in the first sentence of a paragraph.

2. Sometimes the topic sentence is the last sentence in a paragraph. When the first sentence doesn't tell you the main idea, look at the last sentence in the paragraph and see if it's there.

3. In some paragraphs, the topic sentence is in the middle of the paragraph. In these paragraphs, you can only find the main idea by reading the paragraph carefully and figuring out what the paragraph is telling you.

4. In some paragraphs, there is no topic sentence. The main idea is not stated clearly in any one sentence of the paragraph. Often this happens when the main idea has already been stated in another paragraph. When this happens, you really have to read carefully to see if you can figure out what the paragraph is trying to tell you.

HOW TO READ FOR MEANING

Reading for meaning means finding the main idea and supporting details in your reading. You can read for meaning by using these four steps:

SURVEYING
READING
MAPPING
CHECKING YOURSELF

83

6. Have your students read *How Do You Find The Main Idea?* (page 83). Discuss for clarity and emphasis.

4-6 minutes

You may need to devote an entire period to directions #2 - #6 above and complete this unit on the following day. However, if your students are competent at working with these concepts and skills, you may want to complete the unit in one period. If your students are having more difficulty than you anticipated with these concepts and skills, you may want to switch to the Second Alternative.

7. Have your students work through *How To Read For Meaning* (pages 83-86) in a way that is appropriate for your class. You may want to lead them through each step of the *Reading for Meaning* method. Or you may want to introduce the method to your students, lead them through the first step (*surveying* and Exercise IV on page 84), and then have them work through the remaining steps on their own. If you do the latter, go over Exercises IV - VI (pages 84-86) when your students have completed them.

For Exercise IV, be sure to give your students only 20-25 seconds to survey the paragraph. Then ask them to write the main idea.

20-40 minutes

STEP #1: SURVEYING

When you first start to read a paragraph, don't read it word for word. Instead *SURVEY* the paragraph first.

SURVEYING means to look quickly at any heading or titles over the paragraph and then read the first and last sentences. *SURVEYING* will usually let you find out what the paragraph is about. And it takes only a minute or less!

EXERCISE IV

Directions: *SURVEY* the paragraph below. On the lines below it, write what you think the *main idea* of this paragraph is.

A PROFIT IN FROGS

People don't usually think of frog raising as a profitable business, but many people are willing to pay for frogs. Universities and high schools buy frogs for use in their science labs. Restaurants will pay $4.50 or more for a pound of dressed frog meat, as frogs are considered a delicacy by many people. NASA uses frogs in space and will pay $25 or more for a healthy bullfrog. Probably more frogs have orbited the earth than people. People who own ponds will also buy frogs because frogs can help to keep down the insect population. So, the next time that you think about leaving a frog in your teacher's desk, you may decide that there's a more profitable use for your hopping, green friend.

_____

_____

STEP #2: READING

Once you've *SURVEYED* a paragraph, you usually have a sense of what the *main idea* is. Now *READ* the paragraph at your normal rate of reading. As you *READ,* look for SUPPORTING DETAILS that prove, explain, or tell you more about the main idea.

EXERCISE V

Directions: Read the paragraph about "A Profit In Frogs." As you read, be sure to look for supporting details. List at least two details on the lines below.

_____

_____

84

153

STEP #3: MAPPING

    MAPPING is a way of taking notes about your reading. Look at the *MAP* below for the paragraph about frogs.

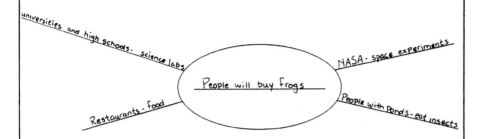

You can take *MAPPING* notes in this way:

1. First write the MAIN IDEA on a line in the middle of your paper. Then circle the MAIN IDEA.

2. List each SUPPORTING DETAIL that you find on a line that touches the circle around the MAIN IDEA.

    MAPPING is a way of taking notes that helps you to understand what the main idea is and what the supporting details are.

EXERCISE VI

Directions: Survey the paragraph below. Then read it and take notes in the *MAP* below the paragraph.

SMART CHIMPS!

Chimpanzees are among the most intelligent animals on earth other than human beings. The structure or makeup of the chimpanzee brain is a lot like the structure of the human brain. Chimps have the ability to use simple tools. In recent years, scientists have found that chimps communicate with each other through noises and gestures. Chimps also seem to be able to learn words and make signs that stand for words.

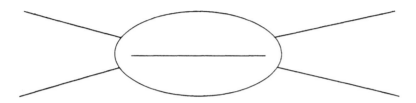

STEP #4: CHECKING YOURSELF

Now, look at your mapping notes and *CHECK YOURSELF*. Using only your notes, tell yourself what the reading is about. Or tell someone who hasn't read the paragraph.

When you take a little time to CHECK YOURSELF, you'll see what you have learned. And you'll find it much easier to remember what you have read.

86

155

EXERCISE VII

Directions: Go back and look through the four steps. They are these:

SURVEYING
READING
MAPPING
CHECKING YOURSELF

Then use the four steps to *read for meaning* the three paragraphs on this page and the next.

VISITORS FROM OUTER SPACE

You may not believe in extra-terrestrial life forms, but the fact is that we get "visitors" from outer space daily. Each year at least 20,000 tons of material from meteors enters our atmosphere. This means about 50 tons a day! Chances of the meteors being big enough to cause us any harm are incredibly slim. The earth's atmosphere burns up the material from outer space before it can reach the surface of the earth. Only 10 to 20 new meteors are actually found on the earth's surface each year. But as they enter the earth's atmosphere, the burning can be seen from earth as a streak of light. So, we should be able to locate "a falling star" on any clear night.

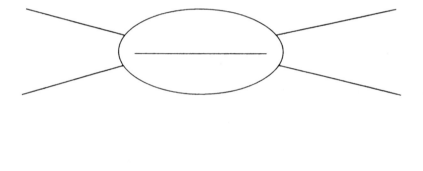

8.   Omit Exercise VII.

THE WORLD HAS BEEN ROUND FOR A LONG TIME!

Some say that Columbus discovered that the world was round. This is not entirely true. Many people knew the world was round long before the days of Columbus. The Greek mathematician, Pythagoras, declared that the world was round in the sixth century B.C. Hundreds of years before the birth of Christ, Eratosthenes figured the distance around the world. During the same time period, Aristotle reported rumors of lands on the other side of the globe. The Greek map maker, Strabo, wrote of men's attempts to sail around the world in the 7th century A.D. Many well educated men of Columbus's day agreed with Columbus that it was perfectly possible to reach the east by sailing west because the earth was a sphere. So, you see, the idea that the earth is round has been around for a long time.

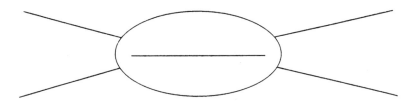

THE GENTLE APE

It's hard to imagine any relative of King Kong as being gentle. But according to Dr. Francine Paterson, the 230 pound Koko is just that. Koko is a lowland female gorilla who has been working with Dr. Paterson for over a decade. By the use of sign language, Koko let Dr. Paterson know that she wanted a kitten for her birthday. When Paterson gave her a little kitten, Koko was delighted. She spent many hours playing with the tiny animal, carrying her kitten from place to place, gently stroking its fur, and bending over to give it a kiss. When the kitten died, Koko was struck with deep grief. It wasn't until the kitten was replaced that Koko resumed her normal activities. It might also interest you to know that Koko is a vegetarian. She obviously prefers petting small creatures to eating them!

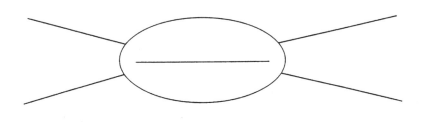

88

157

WHY TAKE NOTES?

"Taking notes is a lot of work. Why bother?"

Have you ever said this? Or heard a friend say it? Well, why should you take notes? Here are two good reasons for taking notes:

1. When you take notes, you learn by writing the main idea and supporting details down on your paper. You'll understand your reading better if you take a few minutes to write down your notes. You'll also remember the main idea and supporting details better.

2. When you take notes, you have a record of what you've read. You can use the record to study for tests.

89

9. Have a student read aloud *Why Take Notes?* (page 89). Discuss for clarity and emphasis.

5-8 minutes

UNIT VII SUMMARY: READING FOR MEANING

READING FOR MEANING means locating *main ideas* and the important *supporting details* in your reading.

The *main idea* in a paragraph is the most important idea. It is the idea that the rest of the paragraph is about.

Supporting details explain, prove, or tell something more about the main idea. They make the main idea more clear or give more information about it.

The main idea of a paragraph is often stated in the *topic sentence*. Most often the topic sentence is the first sentence in the paragraph. It can also be the last sentence or in the middle of the paragraph.

How do you READ FOR MEANING? Use these four steps:

1. SURVEYING: Look quickly at any headings or titles above the paragraph. Then read the first and last sentences of the paragraph. SURVEYING will usually help you find out what the *main idea* is.

2. READING: Read the paragraph at your normal rate of reading. As you read, look for *supporting details*.

3. MAPPING: Make a map like the one below to take notes from your reading. MAPPING helps you to learn the *main idea* and *supporting details* of the reading. It also gives you a record of the reading that you can use later.

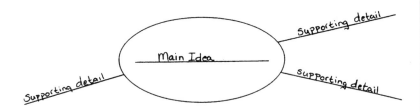

4. CHECKING
   YOURSELF: Look at your MAPPING notes and tell yourself what the reading is about. Or ask yourself: what have I learned from reading this?

90

Second Alternative

1-3. Follow the directions as they are listed in the *First Alternative.*

4. Read aloud *Reading For Meaning* (page 78), or have a student read it aloud. Discuss briefly for emphasis. Then do Exercise I (page 79) together. Discuss how some likely suggestions for the main idea, such as "how dogs smell," "kinds of dogs," "dogs help humans," and so on are really not the main idea.

    10 minutes

5. Read aloud *Main Idea And Supporting Details* (page 80), or have a student read it aloud. Have your students do Exercise II (page 80). Discuss your students' answers.

    10 minutes

6. Have your students do Exercise III (pages 81-82). Discuss your students' answers.

    10-15 minutes

7. Have a student read aloud *How Do You Find The Main Idea?* (page 83), or read it yourself. Discuss by reviewing *PARAGRAPHS A-D*. Point out that in *PARAGRAPH A,* the topic sentence is at the beginning of the paragraph. In *PARAGRAPH B* the topic sentence is at the end of the paragraph. In *PARAGRAPH C* the topic sentence is in the middle of the paragraph. In *PARAGRAPH D* there is no clearly defined topic sentence.

    5-10 minutes

    Over the next few days in class you'll want to reinforce your students' understanding of main ideas, supporting details, and topic sentences by having your students identify these elements in paragraphs from your own textbooks and/or other reading. When your students have gained competence in working with these concepts and skills, continue this unit with #8 below.

8. Have your students work through *How To Read For Meaning* (pages 83-86) in a way that is appropriate for your class. You may want to lead them through each step of the *Reading For Meaning* method. Or you may want to introduce the method to your students, lead them through the first step (*surveying* and Exercise IV on page 84), and then have them work through the remaining steps on their own. If you do the latter, go over Exercise IV-VI (pages 84-86) when your students have completed them.

    For Exercise IV, be sure to give your students only 20-25 seconds to survey the paragraph. Then ask them to write the main idea.

    20-40 minutes

9. Have a student read aloud *Why Take Notes?* (page 89). Discuss for clarity and emphasis.

5-8 minutes

10. If your students can benefit from more practice of the concepts and skills introduced in this unit, have them do Exercise VII (pages 87-88). You may want to do this in class and give your students immediate feedback about their work. Or you may want to have them complete this exercise for homework. If your students do the exercise for homework, go over their answers the next day in class.

20-30 minutes

ANSWERS FOR EXERCISES IN UNIT VII

Page 79: Exercise I

PARAGRAPH A

Dogs have a strong sense of smell and can use it for tracking.

Page 80: Exercise II

PARAGRAPH A

Supporting details:

1. Tracking by smell, dogs can find people who are lost in the woods.

2. Dogs can track prey for hunters.

3. Some dogs are better than others at tracking by smell.

Pages 81-82: Exercise III

PARAGRAPH B

Main Idea:

Ben Franklin was a man of many talents.

Supporting details:

1. Ben Franklin organized many institutions.

2. He organized the first American expedition to the Arctic.

3. He invented many useful things.

4. He wrote books and newspapers.

5. He took part in the politics of early America.

PARAGRAPH C

Main Idea:

"Lucy" can be described from the bones they found.

Supporting details:

1. Lucy was an Hominindae.

2. She had a skeleton much like ours.

3. She stood three feet, eight inches and weighed 65 pounds.

4. She had great muscular strength.

5. She had a large, apelike face.

6. She had a small brain.

PARAGRAPH D

Main Idea:

Killer whales communicate with each other.

Supporting details:

1. clicks tell where food located

2. whistles for socializing

3. screams different within each pod

4. whales may have dialect

Page 84: Exercise IV

People will buy frogs.

Page 84: Exercise V

See page 85 in **Student Text.**

Page 86: Exercise VI

Structure of chimp brain like human brain

Chimps use simple tools

Chimps are very smart animals

chimps communicate with noises, gestures

Chimps can understand spoken words

Meteors from Outer Space

- each year 20,000 tons - 50 tons a day
- earth's atmosphere burns them up
- We can see "falling stars" meteors on clear nights
- 10-20 new meteors found each year

Knowledge of Round World

- Pythagoras - Greek Mathematician declared earth round 6th century B.C.
- Before Christ's birth - Eratosthenes figured distance around world
- Many educated men of Columbus' day believed earth round
- Strabo - Greek Map-Maker 7th century A.D. wrote of attempts to sail around the world

Koko - Gentle Ape

- Koko 230 lb. female gorilla
- wanted kitten for her birthday
- Koko vegetarian
- was very upset when kitten died

PLEASE NOTE: These answers are only "suggested." Accept any answers that are accurate and make sense. Encourage the use of abbreviations and pictures.

ADDITIONAL SUGGESTIONS

1. A good source book for teaching about main ideas is *Getting the Main Idea, Specific Skill Series* (Barnell Loft, 1999). Another useful resource is *Main Idea Set* by Ward Beech (Stech Vaughn, 1997).

2. You can create activities that require your students to read for main ideas:

    a. Cut out interesting newspaper articles without the headlines: ask your students to create headlines for these articles.

    b. Cut out newspaper articles and their headlines. Put the articles in one box and the headlines in another. Ask your students to match the articles with their headlines.

    c. Have your students create ads for certain products. Tell them that they must write and design the ads so that the most useful aspects of the product are stressed.

    d. Have your students view a short segment of "Sesame Street." Tell them beforehand that they are going to be looking for the teaching or main idea behind each skit, so they don't think they are being asked to do a childish task. Discuss the main ideas and how they were illustrated.

3. Give your students topic sentences that summarize parts of a lesson or a unit you have taught. Ask your students to state the main ideas expressed in the topic sentences and supply the supporting details in mapping form. Students can do this kind of exercise individually or in groups.

4. Give your students practice in paraphrasing main ideas. You can do this in the following ways:

    a. Examine topic sentences of paragraphs. (You can use the paragraphs from this unit.) Have the students rewrite the topic sentences without changing the meaning. For example, "Killer whales communicate with each other" could be rewritten "Killer whales send messages to other killer whales."

    b. Have students retitle headlines, article titles, or chapter headings.

    c. Give your students paragraphs at a higher reading level with the topic sentences underlined. Have the students rewrite these topic sentences "in their own words." You may have to give them some help with the content for them to be able to do this.

5. Review Unit I: WAYS TO LISTEN. Do the same kind of activity as the one in this unit, but ask your students to listen for main ideas and supporting details. You may even want to make a game of this by offering so many points for a correctly stated main idea and points for details.

6. Keep a classroom wall chart for abbreviations, and have students make a similar chart of their own. Encourage regular additions to each chart.

    Examples:

    | + | .... | and |
    | w | .... | with |
    | → | .... | causes, leads to |

UNIT VIII: TAKING NOTES—MAPPING AND OUTLINING

This unit continues the sequence begun in Unit VII by focusing your students' attention on note taking as an important skill in itself. Again we urge you to look at these three units together and adapt them to the needs of your students. These skills for taking notes are best learned when they are reinforced through regular practice in the context of your ongoing curriculum. You may want to develop a note taking system as suggested in Unit IX to give your students a practical application of the skills learned in these units.

We strongly believe that the measure of a student's note taking capability is not the particular method employed but, rather, the usefulness of the student's notes to that student. Research into cognitive and learning styles during the past three decades has verified what every perceptive classroom teacher already knows: that people perceive, understand, and respond to the world in different and personal ways. This diversity in learning style argues for diverse methods for taking notes. The activities in this unit introduce your students to three different note taking methods: mapping; mapping with numbers; and outlining.

The unit also suggests that (1) different individuals may use different methods in the same situation and that (2) any one student may want to use different note taking methods in different situations. For example, a student who works well with linear, sequential processes may feel more comfortable and be more effective with outlining. A more visually oriented student, however, may flourish with the use of mapping. Also, even the most sequentially oriented student may find mapping valuable in a particular context, and vice versa.

This diversity in learning style also informs us that for any particular note taking situation, there may not be a "correct" set of notes. Instead, students may include a similar body of main ideas and important details but record them in very different ways. In giving your students feedback about their note taking skills, we suggest that you primarily consider the effectiveness of your students' notes for them as individuals.

During our classroom testing of this unit, some teachers reported that their students found outlining a difficult task. If your students experience this, you may want to have them work with partially completed outlines at first. Then you can gradually reduce what is supplied in the outline until the students are creating their own outlines.

A resource for additional practice in mapping and graphing data is Graphic Organizers — Helping Children Think Visually by Kris Flynn (Creative Teaching Press, 1995).

UNIT VIII: TAKING NOTES — MAPPING AND OUTLINING

INTRODUCTION

In the unit about READING FOR MEANING, you learned about *mapping* as a way of taking notes. This unit will help you to learn more about how to use *mapping*. It will also help you to learn about another way of taking notes called *outlining*.

> **REMEMBER:** Taking notes helps you to learn more about what you are reading or hearing. Also, when you take notes, you have a record to study when you have a test.

TIPS FOR TAKING NOTES

1. Your notes are for you! Take notes that make sense to you. This means that you can use words from your reading, too, but be sure you understand what your notes say.

2. When you take notes, you don't need to write in complete sentences. Write down only the words and phrases that tell you the main ideas and important details in your reading. You can also use abbreviations and symbols.

3. Don't write down everything in your reading. Write down only the main ideas and important details in your notes.

SUGGESTED DIRECTIONS FOR UNIT VIII

1. Read the *Introduction* (page 91) aloud to your students. Then have a student read aloud each of the *Tips For Taking Notes* (page 91). Discuss each tip for clarity and emphasis.

   Approximate time: 5 minutes

BREAKING DOWN SENTENCES

When you take notes, you want to write as few words as possible that tell the important ideas and information. One way to do this is *breaking down* the sentences in your reading into a few key words.

Look at the sentence below:

In 1977 *Star Wars*, a movie that was directed by George Lucas, who had graduated from a California film school only a few years earlier, began to play in theaters all over the country with great success.

Now, look at an example of the notes from this sentence:

1977 — *Star Wars* — great success — by George Lucas.

When you break down a sentence, try to write as few words as you can. But be sure to keep the important ideas and information.

EXERCISE I

Directions: Read the sentences below. *Break down* each into as few words as possible that tell the important ideas and information.

1. The stories of Greek myths make good reading, for the gods and goddesses are dramatically filled with human emotion: love, hate, and jealousy.

   _____

2. Energy that was created from wind power could save the states of the windy north from their need to burn fuel.

   _____

3. The apple, the delicious fruit of the Garden of Eden, is an important fall harvest for the state of New York.

   _____

4. In the late eighteen forties many people made a mad dash to California hoping to get rich through the discovery of gold.

   _____

5. The fair-haired, tall, and hard fighting sailor of Scandinavia was known as the Viking.

   _____

92

2. Have your students read *Breaking Down Sentences* (page 92), or read it aloud to them. Discuss briefly. Have the students do Exercise I (page 92). Go over the exercise.

5-10 minutes

NOTE: Your students may need more work in *Breaking Down Sentences*. If this is the case, give them additional practice with other sentences before you move on.

EXERCISE II

Directions: Read the paragraph below using the four steps you learned in the last unit. Do you remember them?

SURVEYING

READING

MAPPING

CHECKING YOURSELF

Also use the *Tips for Taking Notes* that you read on page 91 in this unit.

Sioux Indian children were taught to swim at a very early age. When the baby was two months old, its mother would take it to a quiet spot along the river bank. She would place her hands gently under the baby's belly and place him or her into the shallow, warm water until it came up around him or her. Then suddenly the baby's sturdy legs would begin to kick and his or her arms to whip through the water. The next time the baby lasted a little longer, and by the third or fourth time the mother could take her hands away for a bit while the baby held his or her head up and dogpaddled for himself or herself.

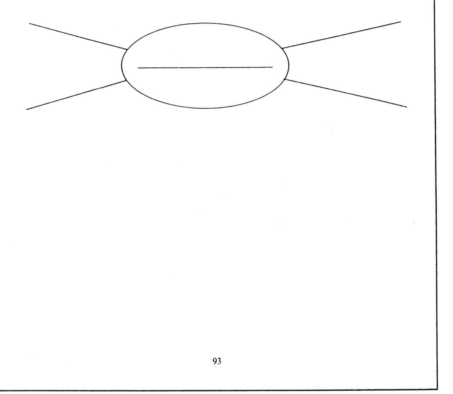

93

3. Have your students do Exercise II (page 93). Then go over the exercise. (Before your students begin, you may want to review the *reading for meaning* method with them.)

    PLEASE NOTE: A completed map for this exercise appears on page 94.

    5-10 minutes

ANOTHER WAY TO TAKE NOTES: MAPPING WITH NUMBERS

You may have had some difficulty in drawing up your MAP for the paragraph about the Sioux baby. Maybe you asked yourself questions like these:

How do I know which line I should start with?

Can any detail go on any line? Or is there a place where each one belongs?

When the reading about which you are taking notes is organized in a certain order or sequence, you can still use a kind of MAPPING for your note taking. You do this by numbering the *supporting details* on your MAP. The details show the order of the sequence.

Look at the map below, and you'll see an example of MAPPING WITH NUMBERS.

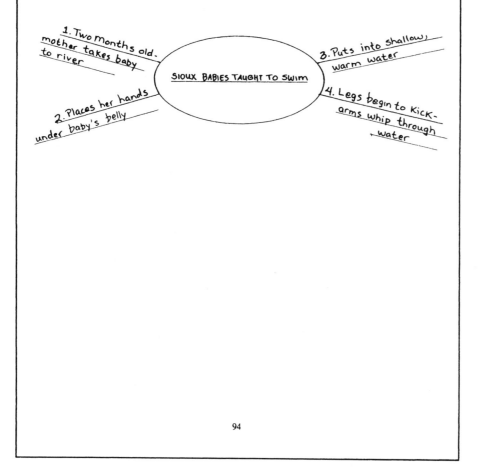

94

4. Read aloud *Another Way To Take Notes: Mapping With Numbers* (page 94), or have students read it aloud. Look at the example together, and discuss for clarity and emphasis. Discuss when this way of taking notes might be useful. Then have your students do Exercise III (page 95). Go over the exercise. Or you may want to do Exercise III on the board as a whole class activity.

10 minutes

170

EXERCISE III

Directions: Try to map the paragraph below by MAPPING WITH NUMBERS.

In its short lifetime, the butterfly goes through four complete changes. We can call these changes "Stages of Life for the Butterfly." The first stage is the egg stage. The adult female chooses a good food source to lay her eggs on. The second stage is the larvae or caterpillar stage. When the eggs hatch, the hungry caterpillars soon devour the leaves around them. They need to eat a lot because they don't eat at all in their third stage, and many don't eat in the fourth stage. Their third stage is spent resting in a cocoon or pupa chrysalis. Finally the adult emerges from the cocoon. In the last stage of life, the butterfly's main job is to mate and lay eggs.

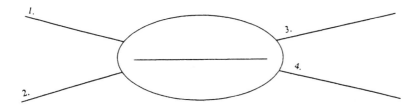

95

A THIRD WAY TO TAKE NOTES: OUTLINING

When a paragraph is organized into a certain sequence of events, it is easy to use a third way of taking notes called OUTLINING. This is much the same as MAPPING WITH NUMBERS, but the way the information is set up is different.

Look below, and you'll see the form for OUTLINING.

OUTLINE FORM

I. Main Idea

    A. Supporting detail

    B. Supporting detail

    C. Supporting detail

HOW TO OUTLINE

1. Use a Roman numeral to list main ideas.

2. Use capital letters to list supporting details. Indent each capital letter a little way to the right of the Roman numeral.

EXERCISE IV

Directions: Write your notes about the butterfly in the outine form below.

I. _____

    A. _____

    B. _____

    C. _____

    D. _____

5. Read aloud *A Third Way To Take Notes* (page 96), or have students read it aloud. Discuss for clarity and emphasis. Discuss when this way of taking notes might be useful. Then have your students do Exercise IV (page 96). Go over the exercise. Again you may want to do this as a class activity.

5-10 minutes

6. Have your students do Exercise V (page 97). Go over the exercise. (You may want to do this exercise as a whole class activity.)

7. Have your students read *How Should You Take Notes?* (page 97). Discuss for clarity and emphasis.

UNIT VIII SUMMARY: TAKING NOTES—MAPPING AND OUTLINING

Three good ways of taking notes are: OUTLINING
                                        MAPPING
                                        MAPPING WITH NUMBERS

OUTLINING

I. Main Idea

      A. Supporting detail
      B. Supporting detail
      C. Supporting detail
      D. Supporting detail

MAPPING

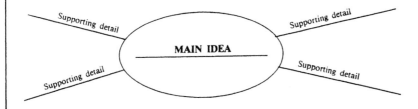

MAPPING WITH NUMBERS

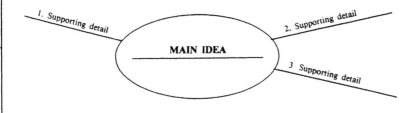

ANSWERS FOR EXERCISES IN UNIT VIII

Page 92: Exercise I

1. Greek myths - good reading - gods and goddesses filled with human emotion
2. Northern states - wind energy can save fuel needs
3. Apple - important fall harvest in NY
4. Late 1890s people went to CA seeking gold
5. Viking - Scandinavian sailor and fighter

Page 93: Exercise II

Answers are on page 94 in the **Student Text** (omit the numbers for this exercise).

Page 95: Exercise III

1. Egg Stage - eggs laid on food source

2. Caterpillar Stage - caterpillars eat

Life Stages of Butterfly

4. Adult butterfly - lays eggs

3. Cocoon Stage - Resting

Page 96: Exercise IV

1. Life Stages of the Butterfly

    A. Egg Stage - eggs laid on food source
    B. Caterpillar stage - caterpillars eat
    C. Cocoon stage - resting
    D. Adult butterfly stage - lays eggs

Page 97: Exercise V

1. Causes of Hail

    A. Hot air, thunderstorm
    B. Cold air over warm air - upward wind
    C. Rain blown up into cold air
    D. Rain freezes - hail
    E. Hail blown down, up many times before it hits the ground

ADDITIONAL SUGGESTIONS

1. Have your students use their note taking skills in as many different contexts as possible. For example, have students map or outline sections of a textbook. Help your students build their note taking skills gradually and thoroughly. Be careful to assign materials well within their reading levels while your students are still learning mapping and outlining methods.

2. Collect and review the notes that your students take. If at all possible, conference with the students individually about their progress.

3. Have your students map or outline a process that they know well. For example: baking a cake, building a model, setting up a tent, or getting ready to come to school. This kind of exercise will also reinforce sequencing skills and the selection of main ideas.

4. Ask your students to map or outline a descriptive paragraph. For example, have them map the traits of a main character or the main parts of a flower. By doing this sort of exercise, your students will discover that the sequence of a map or outline can vary in many situations and still be valid.

5. After practice with short selections, go on to mapping or outlining more information such as a page of material, a chapter of a textbook (make sure you pick a text with distinct headings), or the plot of a well known tale.

6. Have the students map a geographical map, a picture, or any other visual aid. For example, if you are doing a unit on Native Americans, you could have your students make an outline or map of the different kinds of shelter based on pictures of tipis, long houses, cliff dwellings, and so on.

UNIT IX: LISTENING AND TAKING NOTES

This unit provides an experience for your students to integrate listening skills with note taking skills.

For Exercises I and II in this unit, we have asked you (1) to create and deliver a short talk and (2) to structure and lead a brief class discussion. We have not provided the content for these exercises because we are certain that what you can create for these purposes will be more engaging and useful to your students than what we can provide for you. We suggest that you create content for these activities that is an integral part of your ongoing curriculum.

Before you begin this unit, we also suggest that you review Additional Suggestions #1-3. These suggestions are especially important for a group of students that has not had much experience with note taking. Students need to perceive the importance of developing a system of taking notes and of discussing these skills in class. They will make more sense of these skills if the skills are practiced within your curriculum. Additional Suggestions #1 and #2 offer specific suggestions for the practice of these skills.

PLEASE NOTE: With some classes you will want to consider teaching UNIT XI: ORGANIZING IDEAS prior to this unit. The activities in Unit XI will focus your students on key note taking concepts: topic, main idea, and supporting details.

UNIT IX: LISTENING AND TAKING NOTES

INTRODUCTION

In the previous two units, you learned about three ways of taking notes:

outling
mapping
mapping with numbers

You have already used two of these note taking methods to take notes from reading. These methods can be useful to you in many other ways. One of these ways is taking notes from listening.

This unit will give you practice in listening and taking notes.

LISTENING AND TAKING NOTES

Much of what you need to learn to do well in any class will be covered in the class itself. One way to learn more in class is to take notes.

Taking *brief* notes in class can help you learn in the following ways:

1. Taking notes in class can help you to find the main ideas of what is being said, because you'll only want to write down the main ideas.

2. Writing down the main ideas as notes will help you to learn them better.

3. When you take notes in class, you can use your notes later to study for a test.

99

SUGGESTED DIRECTIONS FOR UNIT IX

1. Have your students read the *Introduction* and *Listening And Taking Notes* (page 99). Discuss briefly.

   Approximate time: 5 minutes

2. Read aloud *How Do You Start?* (page 100). Discuss for clarity and emphasis. Have a different student read each of the *Tips For Taking Notes From Listening* (page 101). Briefly discuss each tip.

5-10 minutes

179

TIPS FOR TAKING NOTES FROM LISTENING

1. Be an *active* listener! Try to make sense of what the speaker is saying. Try to connect what the speaker is saying with what you already know.

2. If you can, "picture" in your mind what is being said.

3. Before you start to take notes, think about how the speaker has organized what he or she will say. For example, is there an outline on the board? Is it a class discussion? Then decide what method you want to use to take notes.

4. Try to spend most of your time listening. Figure out what the main ideas are, and write them down. Use only words and phrases, not complete sentences. Remember: your notes are for you; make sure they make sense to you!

5. When your teacher tells you that you'll need to know something, be sure to write it down.

101

EXERCISE I

Directions: Your teacher will give a talk for a few minutes. Take notes from the talk in the space below.

102

3.   Have your students read the directions for Exercise I (page 102). Put a brief outline for a five minute talk on the board. Then ask your students to decide what method they plan to use for taking notes from your talk. Deliver your talk to the class while your students take notes.

8-10 minutes

LOOKING AT YOUR NOTES

Directions: Look carefully at your notes from Exercise 1. Then answer the questions below.

1. What note taking method did you use? _____

_____

2. How well did this method work for you? _____

_____

_____

3. Do your notes make sense to you? _____

_____

4. How could you make your notes better or more helpful to you? _____

_____

_____

103

4. Have your students answer the questions in *Looking At Your Notes* (page 103). Discuss each of the questions with your students. You may want to have several of your students put their notes on the board.

8-10 minutes

EXERCISE II

Directions: Your teacher will lead a short class discussion. Take notes from the discussion in the space below.

104

5. Have your students read the directions for Exercise II (page 104). Ask your students to decide which note taking method they plan to use. Then lead a five minute class discussion. You will want to remind your students that they will need to participate in the discussion and take notes about it.

   8-10 minutes

LOOKING AGAIN AT YOUR NOTES

Directions: Look carefully at your notes from Exercise II. Then answer the questions below.

1. Did you use the same note taking method that you used for Exercise I?

    _____

2. Explain why you chose the method that you used. _____

    _____

    _____

    _____

3. How is taking notes during a class discussion different from taking notes during a lecture?

    _____

    _____

4. Do your notes make sense to you? _____

5. How could you make your notes better or more helpful to you?

    _____

    _____

105

6. Ask your students to evaluate their own notes by answering the questions in *Looking Again At Your Notes* (page 105). Discuss their answers.

    5-10 minutes

UNIT IX SUMMARY: LISTENING AND TAKING NOTES

Much of what you need to learn for any class will be covered in the class itself. Taking *brief* notes in class can help you with this learning.

Use a note taking method with which you are comfortable when you start. Later on, you may want to use different methods in different situations. For example:

1. You can use the *outline* method for any kind of organized talk. You can also use *mapping with numbers* for an organized talk.

2. You can use the *mapping* method or *mapping with numbers* for taking notes during a less organized activity, such as a class discussion.

Be an *active* listener! Try to make sense of what the speaker is saying. Spend most of your time listening. Figure out what the main ideas are, and write them down in words and phrases.

REMEMBER: Your notes are for you. Take notes that make sense to you.

106

ADDITIONAL SUGGESTIONS

1. We suggest that you include practice in taking notes from listening as an integral part of your ongoing process of teaching note taking skills. It's crucial that you *both* provide repeated practice for your students *and* give them feedback about the quality of their notes and, thus, the effectiveness of their note taking skills.

2. Note taking involves an integration of many study skills. Many teachers see note taking as a reflection of what is learned daily in the classroom. These teachers also feel that note taking involves an integration of many classroom systems such as being prepared for class, being organized, and having accurate information for homework. For these teachers, taking notes in class is more of a *system* than a *study skill*. If this is the case with your teaching situation, you will want to train your students carefully. A few of the issues you will need to consider are the following:

    a. Why do I want my students to have notes?

    b. Would it be a good idea to require a certain kind of notebook? (For instance, if you want your students to keep class handouts so they can refer to them, it might be a good idea to require a loose leaf notebook.)

    c. Do I want my students to keep different kinds of notes? If the answer is "yes," you will need to help your students set up specific sections of their notebooks.

    d. How can I help my students retrieve information? If you do decide to set up a notebook with your students, it is most important that the students see the worth of keeping a notebook. Young note takers are impressed when they can store, find, and use information that they have recorded.

    e. How will I evaluate my students' notes? Before you test the students on information stored in their notes, you will want to help them evaluate the effectiveness of their notebook organization. Collecting notebooks and commenting on the strengths and weaknesses, quizzing students on the organizational structure, and pairing students so they can compare notes are some of the ways to evaluate the effectiveness of a note taking system.

3. If your students need more direction in taking notes, you may want to create a handout that lists the main ideas of a passage. As you read the passage aloud, have your students note the relevant details and list them under the appropriate main idea. Try this activity with both mapping and outline formats.

UNIT X: IMPROVING YOUR VOCABULARY

Most educators and linguists believe that vocabulary acquisition is encouraged by a wide variety of reading. Also they agree that learning the skills to use context clues significantly aids children in mastering new vocabulary.

Vocabulary lists can be useful. However, the evidence indicates that children can incorporate new words into their vocabulary most effectively if they have seen the words in use.

Units X and XIII deal with vocabulary building skills. This unit focuses on two kinds of skills:

1. developing the student's ability to recognize the context in which words appear in writing; and

2. developing the student's ability to recognize context clues and use them for gaining an understanding of unknown or unfamiliar words.

When a child begins to recognize unknown words within their contexts, he or she becomes more aware of acquiring new vocabulary. When a child learns that he or she can often figure out the meanings of unfamiliar words from their contexts, he or she has acquired a powerful tool for increasing his or her vocabulary.

UNIT X: IMPROVING YOUR VOCABULARY

INTRODUCTION

Your vocabulary includes all of the words that you can understand and use in your thinking, speaking, writing, and reading.

Did you know that the average elementary school student increases his or her vocabulary by about 1000 words every year? The average junior high or middle school student increases his or her vocabulary by almost 2000 words each year!

One important way that you learn new words is through your reading. However, when you are reading, there are some problems that you may have in learning about unknown or unfamiliar words.

1. By now, you probably can read quickly enough so that you may skip over words without realizing that you don't understand them.

2. To look up a word in the dictionary, you have to stop reading. This interrupts the flow of your reading.

3. When you use a dictionary, you must be able to choose the correct meaning from all the meanings listed.

This unit and Unit XIII will help you to learn ways to solve these problems.

107

SUGGESTED DIRECTIONS FOR UNIT X

1. Divide your class into small groups of three or four students.

2. Have your students take turns reading sections of the *Introduction* (page 107) aloud to the class, or read it aloud yourself. Then go over the directions to Exercise I (page 108). Read the three paragraphs aloud to your students. Then ask your students to write definitions for the underlined words. You may wish to have them do this individually or in groups.

Approximate time: 10 minutes

EXERCISE 1

Directions: Your teacher will read the three paragraphs below to you. Pay careful attention to the underlined words. Think about the meaning of these words. When your teacher has finished reading, write the definitions of the underlined words on the lines below.

I wish they hadn't been so worried about us. Jeannie and I had only taken the canoe for a quick trip down the lake.

The day had been a breezy and blue one with lots of sunshine. The sunlight gleamed off the *ridges* of the waves. We tried at first to paddle, but the wind was so strong that it controlled our course. Since our paddling was useless, we *eased* ourselves down and rested against the cushions. We didn't know that sitting on the floor of the canoe was the best thing to do to keep the canoe *upright*.

As the wind grew stronger and the waves rose higher, the canoe began to rise and fall. We would be about to topple over the *crest* of a wave when our well-*dispersed* weight would balance us. Then we would slide easily down the watery slope. *Peering* over the boat's edge was like looking down from a roller coaster. We were rising and falling with each huge, rolling wave.

ridges _____

eased _____

upright _____

crest _____

dispersed _____

peering _____

108

189

LEARNING ABOUT NEW WORDS

When you come across an unknown or unfamiliar word in your reading, you can learn its meaning in two ways.

1. You can look up the word in the dictionary.

2. You can often figure out the meaning of a new word by looking carefully at the meaning of the words and phrases around it. This is called getting the meaning from *CONTEXT CLUES*. Some of you may have used this method in Exercise I.

A *context* is the setting in which something is found. For example, a museum is a context in which paintings are displayed. A gym is a context in which people play basketball. You expect to find certain things because of the context.

In language, *context* means the words and sentences around any particular word. *CONTEXT CLUES* are familiar words and phrases in a sentence or paragraph. These are words that you know. From these familiar words, you can often figure out the meaning of an unknown word.

EXAMPLE   Many animals are *extinct*, such as dinosaurs.

extinct means _____

3. Before going over the definitions of the underlined words, have your students turn to *Learning About New Words* (page 109). Read this section aloud to your students, and discuss it as you go along. Go over the example.

5 minutes

4. Turn back to Exercise I. Go over the definitions, and briefly discuss the context clues available for each underlined word in the passage.

5-10 minutes

EXERCISE II

Directions: Read the rest of the story about the canoeing adventure below. When you find a word that stops you because you are not sure of its meaning, underline the word.

I didn't worry. Jeannie and I were both strong swimmers. The shore wasn't very far away if the canoe decided to turn us into the foaming waters. I daydreamed that we were sailors on the ocean, conquerors of the deep. Poseidon, with all his power, could not entice us to his kingdom.

The ride finally stopped on the southwest side of the vast lake. The canoe came to a natural halt where the waters lapped gently against a small island. Suddenly we realized that we could never paddle back against those waves.

We would have to wait. The lake would become still towards evening. Jeannie and I climbed out of the canoe and found a healthy patch of blueberries. While we devoured the blueberries, we felt completely carefree. Neither of us realized that we were in big trouble.

Then I spied my uncle. He came in a motor boat. The boat slapped against the waves and sprayed water high into the air. He had come looking for us, probably half expecting the canoe to be capsized with two victims floating face down beside it. I knew he was relieved that we were alive. I also knew that his relief would soon turn to anger because we had been so foolish and had caused everyone at home to worry. I stood staring at my toes and felt the exhilaration of the day pour out of me.

110

5. Go over the directions for Exercise II (page 110) and Exercise III (page 111) with your students. Then have them work through these exercises in their groups. When the groups have completed both exercises, go over the words they underlined and the definitions they constructed. Focus the discussion on how they used context clues. You may wish to let one group talk about one of its words, a second group talk about another word, and so on.

15-20 minutes

EXERCISE III

Directions: On the lines for the new words below, write the words that you have underlined in the canoeing story. Then try to figure out the meaning of each word that you have listed from its *context clues*. Write your meaning in the space to the right of the word.

NEW WORDS

MEANING

_____   _____

                               _____

_____   _____

                               _____

_____   _____

                               _____

_____   _____

                               _____

_____   _____

                               _____

_____   _____

                               _____

_____   _____

                               _____

_____   _____

                               _____

_____   _____

                               _____

_____   _____

                               _____

111

192

6. Have your students do Exercise IV (page 112) individually. Go over in class. If you lack time for this exercise, you may wish to assign it for homework and go over it the next day.

    10 minutes

HOW CAN YOU LEARN NEW WORDS FROM YOUR READING

1. Keep a special section in your notebook for new words. In this section, write down all the new words that you come across and their meanings.

2. When you come across a word from your reading that you don't fully understand, first try to figure out its meaning from *context clues.*

3. When you can't figure out the meaning of a new word from its *context clues,* you need to look it up in the dictionary to know what the word means.

UNIT X SUMMARY: IMPROVING YOUR VOCABULARY

A context is the setting in which something is found. In language, context means the words and the sentences around any particular word.

Context clues are familiar words and phrases in a sentence or paragraph. From these familiar words, you can often figure out the meaning of an unknown word.

When you come across a new word in your reading, first try to figure out its meaning from its context clues. If you can't, you need to look it up in the dictionary.

113

---

7. Read aloud *How Can You Learn New Words From Your Reading?* (page 113), or have students take turns reading sections aloud. Discuss briefly.

    10 minutes

ANSWERS FOR EXERCISES IN UNIT X

Page 108: Exercise I

ridges - raised lines or strips that are higher than the rest of the substance

eased - moved slowly, gently

upright - erect, right side up

crest - top

dispersed - spread around

peering - looking

Pages 110-111: Exercises II & III

Answers will vary. These are the words likely to be underlined by your students.

conquerors - ones who gain control

Poseidon - God of the sea in Greek mythology

devouring - eating hungrily

spied - spotted

capsized - turned over

exhilaration - feeeling of great excitement

relieved - let go of worry

victim - one who is injured

Page 112: Exercise IV

1.	d	5.	a
2.	c	6.	b
3.	c	7.	d
4.	c	8.	b

ADDITIONAL SUGGESTIONS

1. If your students have difficulty working with context clues, you may want to let them work with the "cloze" procedure. The "cloze" procedure is a method of deleting specific words from a prose passage and then asking the student to supply the missing words.

    Example:

    When you have a cold, it is a good idea to stay home in _____ .
    You should take two aspirin and _____ plenty of liquids.

This kind of exercise gives your students another way of learning about the uses of context clues.

Using the "cloze" procedure, you can review vocabulary words that illustrate content taught in your class. For example, if you are teaching conceptual words such as *democracy, communism, dictatorship,* and so on, you can photocopy a text, blank out the designated words, and have the students use context to fill in the blanks.

You can also use old workbooks to create "cloze" exercises. Simply black out the words that you want your students to add. Or you can use published materials such as *Cloze, Grades 6-8, Comprehension in Context* by George Moore (Didax Publishers, 1997). Another resource for the "cloze" procedure is the software *Missing Links* (Sunburst Publications). There are two versions of this program. One version has text from children's literature. The other allows you to enter your own text. Each version offers several alternatives of the "cloze" procedure.

2. Design exercises using the reading from your curriculum so students can practice decoding words from context. As your students become adept at decoding words by using context, begin to teach them specific context clues. Examples of specific context clues are restating or defining, comparing or contrasting, making inferences, and creating a mood.

3. Use a context clue exercise that employs imaginary words, such as this one. Look at the imaginary words *snire* in the sentences below.

The creature lowered his head, his eyes blazing. He aimed his snire at his enemy and breathed a flame that consumed her in seconds.

You know that a *snire is something* because the creature aimed *it*. But what kind of *thing* is it? Figure out all that you can about the word *snire* from its context. Then write your definition on the lines below.

snire / snĭr n.

_____

_____

_____

When your students are finished, let them share their definitions with each other and discuss the variations. You may also want your students to work this kind of exercise in pairs or small groups.

4. Have your students keep vocabulary notebooks. Tell them they have to enter three to five words each week. They must also enter the context and the definition. They can use outside reading, television, textbooks, or class discussions as sources for words. For this system to work, you must check these notebooks often and establish grading criteria.

5. "Play" the following activity for several minutes for a number of days.

   Give each student a chart listing common prefixes, roots, and suff~xes, such as the chart below. Invite students to create imaginary words that use these prefixes, roots, and auffixes. Once a student has created an imaginary word, have her or him create a written context for the word. Then have students read what they have written. Have other students guess the meanings of the imaginary words. You may want to do this exercise in pairs.

PREFIXES - meaning	ROOTS - meaning	SUFFIXES
PRE- before	SCRIBE, SCRIPT- writing	ER
POST- after	GEN, GENER, GENIT- birth, class	OR
EXTRA- outside	SOLUT- loosen	NESS
IN- not	VIS, VID- see	ENT, ANT
CONTRA- against	TERRA- earth	MENT
CON- with	LATERAL- side	AL
AD- to	HERE- stick	TION
INTER- between	GREG- gather, group	OUS, IOUS
RE- again		
BI- two		
MULTI- many		

6. Read aloud passages with difficult words but with accessible content. Prepare the students to listen for certain words beforehand. Encourage them to use the context of what you have read to decode the meaning of the words. This is also a good way to review the listening skills taught in the first two units of this **Program**.

UNIT XI: ORGANIZING IDEAS

INTRODUCTION

The skills involved in organizing ideas and information are among the most critical taught in school. Many students at this age have difficulty organizing a hierarchy of ideas. It is often hard for them to label and use topics, main ideas, and supporting details. We have found that it is important for students to start with practical applications of the concepts of main ideas and supporting details, such as how items of clothing might be organized in a drawer. Once the student understands this kind of application, he or she is more able to pursue abstract applications.

You may want to spend additional time exploring the kinds of examples suggested in the *Introduction* (page 114).

Exercises I and II are designed to help your students increase their understanding of the relationship between main ideas and supporting details. These activities also give them practice in determining which is which. Your students are presented with the information in several ways:

1. with the main ideas and details highlighted;
2. with just the main ideas highlighted;
3. with just the details highlighted; and
4. with neither highlighted but both contained within the situation.

Students need to sort through the ways the information in each situation is presented, so they can generate usable lists.

Exercises III and IV introduce the concept of topic. Exercise V asks the students to integrate all of these ideas and gain a sense of the relationship among them.

You'll want to read over this unit carefully before you begin. Decide if you want your students to work these activities in small groups, in pairs, or individually. If you have a young class with little experience with this skill, you may want to do this unit as a group lesson. If you decide to do this, you will want to develop exercises that provide individual practice. There are suggestions for further practice in the *Additional Suggestions.*

SUGGESTED DIRECTIONS FOR UNIT XI

1. Read over the *Introduction* (page 114) with your class. Go over the *Example Situation*. Ask the following questions: What is the difference between a main idea and a detail? How can this list help you find groceries in a busy store? Then ask the students if they have any personal systems in which they use a type of category or main idea to organize details.

   Approximate time: 5-10 minutes

EXERCISE 1

Directions: Read the situations below and on page 116. Each situation requires you to make a list so that you can do the work more efficiently.

Make a list that has main ideas for headings. Place the details below the correct main ideas. Your lists should look something like the shopping list on the previous page. Please feel free to shorten the details into notes.

SITUATION A

You have a test for science class tomorrow on animal characteristics. You are required to know the characteristics of *amphibians*, *mammals*, and *birds*.

You must know which of the characteristics below fits with what kind of animal:

       feeds young with mammary glands
       lives in water and on land
       has wings
       reproduces by laying eggs
       reproduces by giving birth to young animal
       has hair
       has gill-breathing larvae
       has hollow bones
       has backbones
       has feathers
       has gelatinous eggs

First write your main ideas. Then organize the list of details in the spaces below. You may use a detail more than once.

MAIN IDEAS: _____ _____ _____

    DETAILS: _____ _____ _____

               _____ _____ _____

               _____ _____ _____

               _____ _____ _____

               _____ _____ _____

               _____ _____ _____

               _____ _____ _____

2.   Read the directions to Exercise I (pages 115-116) together. Do *Situation A* as a whole class. You may want to use an overhead projector or write on the board. As you do this exercise, point out how the details can be shortened into notes. Note that the lists are much easier to read and use than paragraphs. Discuss why this is so.

5-10 minutes

3.   Have the students complete *Situation B.* Go over their answers.

8 minutes

EXERCISE II

Directions: Read Situation A, and follow the directions at the end of the situation. Do the same for Situation B on page 118.

SITUATION A

Before you can get this week's allowance, your parents insist that you do the following chores:

make bed
do pages 3-4 in math
put away clean clothes
mow lawn
dirty clothes in the hamper
Social Studies report on Alaska
clean shelves
rake leaves
read three chapters of *Island of the Blue Dolphin*
wind up hose

In the space below, make lists of all the chores you have to do. Make sure each list has an appropriate main idea for a heading.

MAIN IDEAS: _____ _____ _____

DETAILS: _____ _____ _____

_____ _____ _____

_____ _____ _____

_____ _____ _____

_____ _____ _____

_____ _____ _____

117

4. Have the students complete Exercise II (pages 117-118). Go over their answers.

10 minutes

SITUATION B

You are going on an overnight hike with some of your friends. It is your assignment to bring the following items: pancake mix, candles, *Trivial Pursuit,* dried fruit, matches, muffin mix, comic books, powdered eggs, cards, newspaper (for starting fires), cereal, instant milk, powdered fruit juice, "slam" books, doughnuts.

Guess what three things you are in charge of and create your lists in the space below:

MAIN IDEAS: _____   _____   _____

DETAILS: _____   _____   _____

_____   _____   _____

_____   _____   _____

_____   _____   _____

_____   _____   _____

_____   _____   _____

TOPICS

A *topic* is broader or larger than a main idea. It can include several main ideas.

EXERCISE III

Directions: Read statements #1 - #4 below, and answer the questions on the lines provided.

1. The topic of Situation A in Exercise I (page 115) might be *Living Things* or *Animals.* Is there any other topic these ideas might fit under?

    _____

2. The topic of Situation B in Exercise I (page 116) might be *Presidents,* or *Famous Politicians.* Can you think of any other topic it could be?

    _____

3. The topic of Situation A in Exercise II (page 117) might be *Chores* or *Ways to Earn Money.* Can you think of another topic that would fit these ideas?

    _____

4. The topic of Situation B in Exercise II (page 118) might be *Scout Trips* or *Hiking Plans.* Can you think of another topic that would fit these ideas?

    _____

EXERCISE IV

Directions: Read the lists in #1 below. Create a topic for the main ideas and details in #1, and write it on the line provided. Do the same for #2 and #3 on page 120.

1. | FOOD | FAVORS | ACTIVITIES | TO DO |
    |------|--------|------------|-------|
    | cake | napkins | dance | bake cake |
    | ice cream | honkers | spin the bottle | write invites |
    | "munchies" | place settings | *Trivial Pursuit* | borrow tapes |
    | hamburgers | prizes | egg walk | go shopping |
    | rolls | | charades | get permission |
    | condiments | | | borrow games |
    | brownies | | | bake brownies |

    The topic is _____

119

5. Read aloud *Topics* (page 119). Discuss for emphasis. Then have students do Exercise III (page 119). Have students share their answers.

    6-8 minutes

6. Read the directions for Exercise IV (pages 119-120) aloud. Do #1 as a whole class activity. Have students do #2. Go over their answers. Then have students do #3, and go over their answers.

    7-10 minutes

204

2. EARLY YEARS | EDUCATION | EVENTS LEADING TO FAME

EARLY YEARS	EDUCATION	EVENTS LEADING TO FAME
one of seven	taught by older brother	became leader of Virginia militia
father died when young	no formal schooling	member of the First Continental Congress
favored son	learned surveying	general of Continental Army
raised in Virginia	took over brother's military duties	commander at Valley Forge
took over Mount Vernon at young age	surveyed wilderness of America	defeated British army

The topic is _____

3.

CLIMATE	GEOGRAPHY	PEOPLE	EXPORTS
wet	mountainous	Celtic	potatoes
mean temp 55° F	island	redheads	whiskey
mild winters	bays	Gaelic	crystal
raw winters	hills	English speaking	lace
snow rare	lakes	black haired blue eyed	dishes
	surrounded by: Atlantic Ocean Irish Sea North Sea		

The topic is _____

120

EXERCISE V

Directions: Pick a topic from the suggestions below. Circle the topic. Then in the spaces below, write out *three* lists showing main ideas and details that fit with this topic.

World War II	Mammals	Famous Authors
Famous Women	Automobiles	Famous Politicians
Vacation spots	Schools	Flight
Television	Technology	Agriculture
Pets	Entertainment	Food
Clothing	Careers	20th Century
Plant Kingdom	Books	Explorers

MAIN IDEAS: _____   _____   _____

DETAILS: _____   _____   _____

_____   _____   _____

_____   _____   _____

_____   _____   _____

_____   _____   _____

_____   _____   _____

121

7. Explain Exercise V (page 121), and have the students complete it for homework. Collect their **Programs**, and give them individual feedback about their lists.

UNIT XI SUMMARY: ORGANIZING IDEAS

A category name is also a *main idea*. The ideas and information within a category are the *details* of that *main idea*.

Details give more information about or support a main idea.

A *topic* is broader or larger than a main idea. It often includes several main ideas.

The chart below shows how these terms are related.

DETAILS
are part of
MAIN IDEAS
are part of
A TOPIC

or

A TOPIC
includes
MAIN IDEAS
are supported by
DETAILS

122

SUGGESTED ANSWERS FOR UNIT XI

Pages 115-116: Exercise I

SITUATION A

amphibians	mammals	birds
lives in water and on land	feeds young with mammary glands	has wings
reproduces by laying eggs	reproduces by giving birth to young animal	has hollow bones
has backbones	has backbones	has backbones
has gill breathing larvae	has hair	has feathers
has gelatinous eggs		

SITUATION B

early years	education	fame
had one sister	walked 3 miles to school	debated Douglas
father Thomas	school for lawyers	captain in Black Hawk War
mother Nancy	trained as clerk	could write well
moved from KY to IL		16th President

Accept any reasonable answers.

Pages 117-118: Exercise II

SITUATION A

school work	house work	yard work
do pps 3-4 math	make bed	mow lawn
SS report - Indians	put away clothes	rake leaves
3 chapters *Island*	clean shelves	wind up hose
	dirty clothes in hamper	

Accept any reasonable answers.

SITUATION B

breakfast food	games	fire materials
pancake mix	*Trivial Pursuit*	candles
dried fruit	"slam" books	matches
muffin mix	cards	newspaper
cereal	comic books	
instant milk		
powdered eggs		
powdered fruit juice		
doughnuts		

Accept any reasonable answers.

Page 119: Exercise III

1. Animal Classifications, Animal Characteristics, Animal Groups

2. Great Americans, American Presidents, Famous Men of the 19th Century

3. Responsibilities, Jobs, Earning My Allowance

4. Camping, Overnight Field Trip, Canoe Trip

Accept any reasonable answers.

Pages 119-120: Exercise IV

1. Party Preparations
2. George Washington
3. Ireland

Accept any reasonable phrasing.

Page 121: Exercise V

Answers will vary.

ADDITIONAL SUGGESTIONS

1. A computer data base is one of the most powerful tools for exploring how ideas and information relate to each other and how you can make hypotheses based on the relationships among ideas and information. Create a computer data base with your students. There are many excellent software programs to help you create a data base. One is Appleworks. Sunburst offers several prepared databases in science and history for students to use. Refer to the following websites for more information:

    www.applestore.com
    www.softseek.com

    When you teach a computer data base, you will want to explain how the terms *file, field,* and *data* replace *topic, main idea,* and *supporting detail.*

    You might enjoy beginning a data base and keeping the records as a class. Topics that lend themselves nicely to a class effort include statistics about the weather, the animal kingdom, and outside reading books. You can use any other topic with which students can do a small amount of research and enter the data on the class data base.

    Good references for data bases include *ClarisWorks for Terrified Teachers* by Terry Rosengart (Teacher Created Materials, 1997) and *PCs for Teachers* by Carol Kellogg (IDG Books Worldwise, 1997).

2. Assign your students a research topic such as "Famous People." As a class, generate the main ideas within the topic. Work with no more than three main ideas at a time. Bring your students to the library, and help them to find supporting details for their main ideas.

3. Introduce content areas by labeling the relevant topic and main ideas that you will be studying. Ask students how many supporting details they already know about each main idea. For example, say:

"We will be studying a topic called *Communities* over the next two weeks. What can you tell me about the following?" (Write on the board.)

COMMUNITIES

RURAL   CITY   SUBURBS   VILLAGE   TOWN

As your students suggest details, write their sugggestions under the appropriate main idea. This is also a good way to design a unit based on what your students already know about a topic.

4. Cut out ads from newspapers and magazines. Have the students place the ads into topics (food). Then have them identify the main idea of each ad (Tasty Pizza) and the supporting details (zesty sauce, choice of topping, delicious cheese, tasty crust).

Suggest a topic such as automobiles, and have your students create their own ads by identifying the main idea (a specific automobile) and supporting details.

UNIT XII: CHARTS — TABLES AND GRAPHS

INTRODUCTION

In school we emphasize the need for students to gain information and solve problems from written text. Yet much of the information available to students, both in and out of school, is presented in some other form than the written paragraph. In many instances, information can be most easily understood when organized and presented pictorially. Graphs, tables, and diagrams can often represent in a single picture what would require many pages of text to describe.

The exercises and the *Additional Suggestions* in this unit are designed to help students develop an understanding of how information is presented in visual ways. The exercises also provide the opportunity for your students to work with some of the skills associated with charts, as described below.

In this unit *chart* is used as a generic term for all such pictorial forms and is defined in the following way: a chart is a picture, graph, or table that shows information in a visual and organized way. Your students will begin to recognize that charts can do the following:

a. help them to *organize* information so that it is more accessible and easier to use;

b. help them to *understand* information better when it is presented in these forms;

c. help them to solve problems; and

d. present information in different ways.

Questions in the exercises of this unit are intended to have students use charts in the following ways:

a. for retrieval of specific information;

b. for comparing and contrasting information;

c. for problem solving involving mathematical calculation;

d. for problem solving involving the drawing of accurate conclusions; and

e. for analyzing how information may best be presented.

It is assumed that your students have gained a basic literacy with tables and graphs prior to their participation in this unit. You may want to review the appropriate chart skills and the terms listed on the next page before starting this unit:

212

grid
horizontal
vertical
axis
percentage
round off
unit
population
sample
poll

In introducing tables and graphs, you will want to avoid complicated explanations. Instead stress the common sense qualities of representing tangible information in this fashion. You might want to introduce this unit by presenting a variety of charts and graphs to your students through use of the overhead projector, bulletin boards, computer programs, and texts. Use sources that make sense to your students, such as community newspapers, illustrations of something you are currently studying, or tables and graphs illustrating personal statistics of the class. See *Additional Suggestions* for more detailed guidelines.

UNIT XII: CHARTS — TABLES AND GRAPHS

INTRODUCTION

A picture or a *chart* can often make clear information that would take many words to explain. For instance, if you were studying the structure of a plant cell, it helps to see a picture of a cell as you are hearing or reading about it.

If you were dividing jobs among the members of the Student Council in order to prepare for a dance, you might make a list or a *table* to show who is on the different committees.

In each of these cases, you are using a *chart* — a kind of picture — to help you understand and organize information. A *chart* can be a diagram, a table, or a graph. Charts are arranged so that you can easily understand and use a lot of information.

Look at the chart of the flower below. It tells you at a glance that a flower is made up of four separate parts. It also tells you what the parts of the pistil and the stamen are and where the parts are in relationship to each other. It would take a great many words to explain these things.

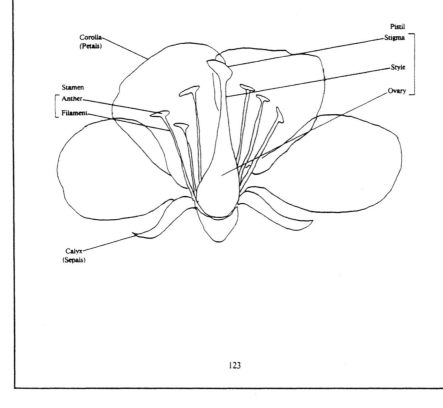

123

SUGGESTED DIRECTIONS FOR UNIT XII

1. Read aloud and discuss the *Introduction* (page 123) with your students. Emphasize the fact that it would take a great many words to explain what the flower charts shows.

   Approximate time: 10 minutes

THREE KINDS OF CHARTS

  In this unit you will be learning about three kinds of charts: *diagrams, tables,* and *graphs.* You will see how they can help you in these ways:

  1. by giving you a "picture" of the information so that the information is easier to *see* and *understand*;

  2. by *organizing* the information so that you can find it more easily; and

  3. by giving you a way to *compare* data or bits of information.

  It is important to understand the kinds of information that diagrams, tables, or graphs present. Then you can use this information to answer questions and solve problems.

124

2. Read *Three Kinds Of Charts* (page 124) aloud to your students, or have a student read it aloud. Discuss briefly.

3-5 minutes

Directions: Read the paragraphs below about volcanoes. Then answer the questions that follow.

THE BIRTH OF A VOLCANO

A volcano is an opening in the earth's surface through which lava, hot gases, and rock fragments burst forward. Such an opening occurs when melted rock from deep within the earth blasts through the surface. Most volcanoes are atop mountains that the volcanoes themselves have created. These mountains (also called volcanoes) are usually cone-shaped mountains that have been built up by lava and other materials thrown out during eruptions.

The volcano actually begins as *magma,* which is melted rock located deep within the earth. At certain depths within the earth, the temperature is so extremely hot that it partly melts the rock inside the earth. When the rock melts, it produces gas that mixes with the magma or melted rock. Most of this magma forms 50 to 100 miles beneath the surface.

The gas-filled magma gradually rises toward the earth's surface because it is lighter than the solid rock around it. As the magma rises, it forms a large chamber in the crust. The crust is the area between the surface of the earth and the earth's mantle. The magma chamber is the holding place from which volcanic materials erupt. Sometimes these chambers are as close as two miles to the surface of the earth.

1. Where is the magma chamber? _____

2. Which is closest to the center of the earth: the crust, the mantle, or the magma chamber?

    _____

3. How is the cone-shaped mountain formed by volcanic forces?

    _____

125

3. Have your students read the directions for Exercise I (page 125) and do the exercise. When they have completed Exercise I, have them turn the page and do Exercise II (page 126). When they have finished Exercise II, discuss how the diagram makes it a great deal easier to answer the questions because it illustrates the text.

10 minutes

EXERCISE II

Directions: Now look at the diagram of the volcano below. First answer questions #1-3, as you did for Exercise I. Then answer #4.

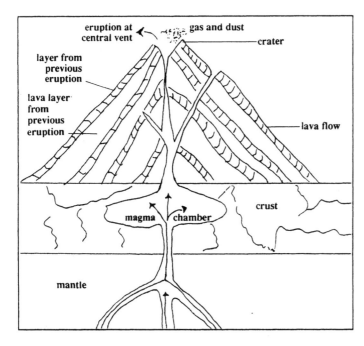

1. Where is the magma chamber? _____

2. Which is closest to the center of the earth: the crust, the mantle, or the magma chamber?

   _____

3. How is the cone-shaped mountain formed by volcanic forces?

   _____

4. Did the diagram help you answer these questions more efficiently? If so, explain how.

   _____

   _____

   _____

126

217

TABLES AND GRAPHS: WAYS TO ORGANIZE INFORMATION

Two other kinds of charts are *tables* and *graphs*. Just like the diagram of a volcano, a table or graph can help you understand much information at a glance. Both tables and graphs are carefully organized to present information in a visual way. You must understand the organization in order to use the information in a table or graph.

127

4. Read aloud *Tables and Graphs: Ways To Organize Information (page 127)*. Discuss briefly.

5 minutes

EXERCISE III

Directions: Now look at the table and the graph below. Although they look different, each is presenting the same information. As you look at this table and graph, try to think of reasons for presenting the information in each way. Then answer the questions that follow on page 129.

TABLE

SPEEDS OF ANIMALS

ANIMAL	MPH	ANIMAL	MPH
cheetah	70	cat	30
lion	50	human	27.89
quarter horse	47.5	elephant	25
cape hunting dog	43	black mumbra snake	20
coyote	43	wild turkey	15
zebra	40	squirrel	12
greyhound	39.35	pig	11
domestic rabbit	35	chicken	9
grizzly bear	30	three-toed sloth	.15

GRAPH

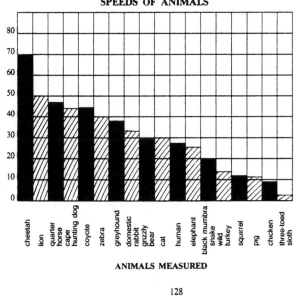

128

5. Have a student read aloud the directions for Exercise III (pages 128-129). Have your students do this exercise and answer the questions. When they have completed the questions, review them. Stress that although these charts present the same information, the emphasis is different.

10 minutes

1. Which chart would be more useful if you wanted to list more information about the speeds of other animals?

   _____

2. Which chart would be more useful to show how impressive the cheetah's running ability was when compared to other animals?

   _____

3. Which chart gives more specific information? _____

4. Which chart makes it easier to see that humans have a low average running ability when compared to other animals?

   _____

DIFFERENT WAYS TO SHOW DIFFERENT KINDS OF INFORMATION

Tables and different kinds of graphs are organized to show different kinds of information.

For example, the table listing speeds of animals shows you specific information organized by how fast each animal runs. The graph shows you the difference in the animals' running speeds. You get a sense of how much faster one animal runs than another.

In the next four exercises, you will be using four different kinds of graphs to help you see and use information. As you learn about each graph, try to notice the particular kind of information that is best shown by that graph.

129

6. Read aloud *Different Ways To Show Information* (page 129). Discuss briefly.

    5 minutes

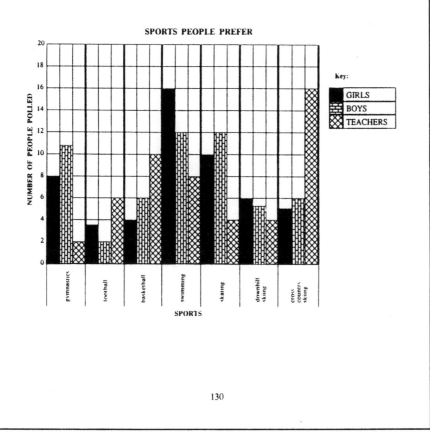

EXERCISE IV: BAR GRAPHS

Directions: Read the information about BAR GRAPHS below. Then study the bar graph and answer the questions on page 131.

A *bar graph* shows information by using different length bars to illustrate a certain amount or number of something. Bar graphs are organized on a grid. This makes it easy to compare one thing to another.

Often several different kinds of bars are used, such as in the example below. This makes it easier to see the different aspects of the things being shown by the graph.

The bar graph below shows the results of a poll taken by a Student Council Committee in the Madville School. This committee asked 50 boys, 50 girls, and 50 teachers what their favorite sports were, so that Madville could develop some afterschool sports activities. They put the information in the form of a bar graph in order to make a presentation to the Student Council.

SPORTS PEOPLE PREFER

NUMBER OF PEOPLE POLLED

Key:
GIRLS
BOYS
TEACHERS

SPORTS

gymnastics football basketball swimming skating downhill skiing cross country skiing

130

7. You can have your students read the directions and do Exercises IV-VII individually or in small groups. When your students have completed each exercise, go over it. In your discussion emphasize how each kind of graph presents information.

You will want to decide the best approach for your class based on how much previous experience your students have had with graphs. If your class is having difficulty with the concepts introduced, you may want to go through each exercise as a class.

20-40 minutes

1. What is the most popular sport at Madville School? _____

   The least popular? _____

2. What sport probably has more girls signing up for it than boys?

   _____

3. Which two populations are the most alike in their choices of favorite sports?

   _____

4. From looking at this poll, there are some indications of the geographical location of the Madville School. Where do you think this school may be located? Why?

   _____

   _____

5. Circle the letter before each of the following ideas that can be represented by creating a *bar graph*.

   a. Number of males and females born in different countries

   b. Percentage of different trees found in a forest

   c. Number of extinct animals found in different countries

   d. How many males and females favor a candidate

   e. How many months with rainfall over three inches

131

EXERCISE V: PICTOGRAPHS

Directions: Read the information below about PICTOGRAPHS. Then study the pictograph below, and answer the questions on page 133.

A *pictograph* is a kind of chart that uses pictures to represent a certain number of something. In a pictograph, a certain amount of something is shown by a picture so that you can easily see how the amounts relate to each other. Pictographs usually are not exact but show amounts that are "rounded off" to the nearest unit.

In the example below, the pictograph shows how much money the Madville student body has earned toward end-of-the-year school trips. Twelve students worked together with a teacher in groups called Teacher Advisories (TA) to earn money. The chart below shows how much money each TA earned. Each $ stands for ten dollars.

$ TOWARDS CLASS TRIPS

Mrs. Arnold's TA	$	$	$						
Ms. Barwin's TA	$	$	$						
Mr. Bolger's TA	$	$	$	$	$	$	$		
Mr. Fotion's TA	$								
Mr. Funzula's TA	$	$	$	$	$	$			
Mr. Kulhowvick's TA	$	$	$	$					
Mr. Rowe's TA	$	$	$	$	$	$	$		
Ms. Ryder's TA	$	$	$	$	$				
Mrs. Sokolich's TA	$	$	$	$	$	$	$	$	$
Ms. Toesing's TA	$	$	$	$					

school goal: $1,000

$ = 10

$ = 5

132

1. What TA has earned the most money so far? _____
   Approximately how much more money has this TA earned than its nearest competitor?

   _____

2. How much money has Ms. Barwin's TA earned? _____

3. How much more money has Ms. Ryder's TA earned than Ms. Arnold's?

   _____

4. How much money have the students earned in total? _____
   Approximately how much more money needs to be earned to reach the school's goals?

   _____

5. Circle the letter before each of the ideas below that you think could be easily represented in a pictograph:

   a. Yearly population of US

   b. Number of hours spent on homework per week

   c. Percentage of time doing daily activities

   d. Number of cars sold by a salesperson per year

   e. Spelling test scores

   f. Number of UFO sightings in Milford, Utah

   g. Number of gallons of milk sold by major companies

133

EXERCISE VI: LINE GRAPHS

Directions: Read the information below about LINE GRAPHS. Then study the line graph below, and answer the questions on page 135.

    Line graphs are useful when you want to look at something to see how it changes under certain measurable conditions, such as over time. Line graphs are also useful when you want to look at the development of similar items so that you can compare them. In the line graph below, for instance, you can see how precipitation changes over a period of time. This line graph also makes it easy to compare rainfall with snowfall.

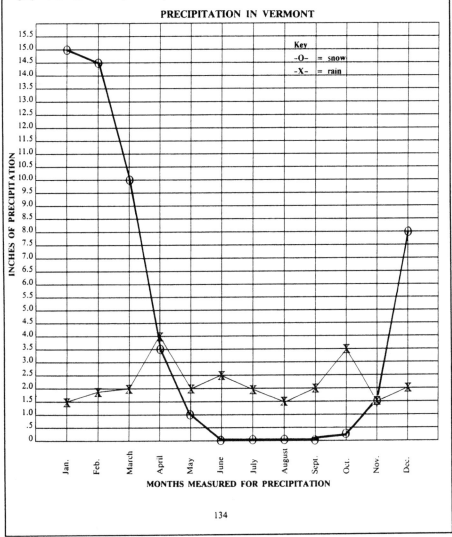

PRECIPITATION IN VERMONT

134

225

1. Name four months when there is no measurable snow in Vermont. _____

   _____

2. Name the three months with the most snow. _____

   _____

3. When might it be best to plan a ski vacation in Vermont? Why? _____

   _____

   _____

4. Name the month when it rains and snows almost the same number of inches.

   _____

5. Circle the letter before each of the ideas below that you think could be easily represented by a line graph:

   a. The yearly earnings of three major companies

   b. Sports people prefer

   c. Yearly number of boy and girl graduates from a certain school

   d. The growth of two similar plants under different conditions

   e. The percentage of people with different racial backgrounds living in the same area

   f. The planets in a solar system

135

EXERCISE VII: PIE GRAPH

Directions: Read the information below about PIE GRAPHS. Then study pie graph below, and answer the questions on page 137.

Below is an example of a *pie graph*. In a pie graph, a circle is used to show the whole amount of something. In the example below, it shows the whole amount of energy sources used in the United States.

The whole is divided into parts that are either fractions or decimals. The parts in this example show what part of all the energy sources are petroleum, natural gas, coal, hydroelectric power, nuclear power, and "other." "Other" shows the combined small amounts of less used energy resources, such as the burning of wood and trash.

A pie graph makes it easy to see the parts of a whole (percentage) and compare them to each other.

SOURCES OF ENERGY CONSUMED IN THE U.S.

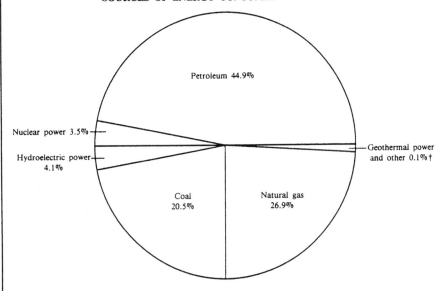

† other includes coke, waste, and wood

1. What are the three most used energy sources in the U.S.? Name them in order from the most to the least. _____

   _____

2. What does "other" include? _____

   _____

3. Which of these energy sources do you consume? _____

4. What does the total circle of this pie graph represent? _____

   _____

5. Circle the letter before each of the ideas below that could be illustrated by a pie chart:

   a. How goods are transported in Canada

   b. Activities that are inexpensive

   c. Speeds of animals

   d. Lists of classmates' birthdays

   e. Number of stars seen from earth

   f. Amount of time spent each day on different activities

UNIT XII SUMMARY: CHARTS — TABLES AND GRAPHS

Charts include diagrams, tables, and graphs. Charts are a good way of showing information. You can learn a great deal just by looking at a chart if you know how to read it.

Each kind of chart can show you different kinds of information:

Diagrams are used to make complicated reading clearer because they *show* you what you are reading about.

Tables show you lists of information, such as who is serving on what committee or the alphabetical list of countries and their populations.

Bar graphs show you information by using different length bars to illustrate a certain amount or number of something. Often more than one kind of bar is used so that you can compare one thing to another.

Pictographs show you information by having a picture represent a certain number of things. For instance, a stick figure could represent 100 human beings. In a pictograph, a certain amount of something is shown by a picture so that you can easily see how different amounts relate to each other. Pictographs usually are not exact but show amounts that are "rounded off" to the nearest unit.

Line graphs show how something changes under certain measurable conditions, such as time. Line graphs are also useful when you want to look at the development of similar items in order to compare them.

Pie graphs make it easy to see the parts of a whole and compare them with each other.

All these kinds of charts can help you to understand and learn important information.

138

8. Read aloud and discuss the *Summary* (page 138).

3-5 minutes

SUGGESTED ANSWERS FOR EXERCISES IN UNIT XII

Page 125: Exercise I

1. The magma chamber is in the earth's crust.

2. The mantle is closest to the center of the earth.

3. The cone-shaped mountain is formed by layers of the lava building up on top of each other.

Page 126: Exercise II

Same answers as Exercise I

4. The diagram helps because it shows you the answers to the questions rather than just explaining them. Accept any reasonable answer.

Pages 128-129: Exercise III

1. The table

2. The graph

3. The table

4. The graph

Pages 130-131: Exercise IV

1. Swimming is the most popular. Football is the least popular.

2. Swimming, football, and downhill skiing have more girls than boys signing up for them.

3. The boys and the girls are the most alike in their choices.

4. This school is located in some northern and mountainous region. You know this because skiing is offered as a choice.

5. a

   d

   e

230

Pages 132-133: Exercise V

1. Mrs. Sokolich's TA $25
2. $25
3. $15
4. $455 $545
5. a

    b

    d

    e

Pages 134-135: Exercise VI

1. June, July, August, September
2. January, February, and March
3. January or February because those are the months with the highest snowfall
4. November
5. a

    c

    d

Pages 136-137: Exercise VII

1. petroleum, natural gas, coal
2. coke, waste, and wood
3. Answers will vary.
4. All sources of energy consumed in the U.S.
5. a

    f

ADDITIONAL SUGGESTIONS

1. The following is an outline of common forms of charts:
   - LISTS
   - TABLES AND SCHEDULES
   - GRAPHS (PICTOGRAPHS, BAR, PIE, LINE or COORDINATE)
   - MAPS
   - DIAGRAMS (PICTURE CHART, DESIGN, SCHEMATIC, FLOW CHART, BLUEPRINT)
   - OTHER SPECIFIC-USE CHARTS (CALENDAR, TIME LINE, CLASS SCHEDULE)

   As an introduction to this unit, you might discuss pertinent charts with your students. You might find it helpful to point out and discuss the following aspects of tables and graphs:

   a. titles and headings

   b. measurement increments (especially on graphs)

   c. organization (especially on lists and tables), such as alphabetical order, ordering from largest to smallest, clustering by attribute (gender, nationality, geographical location), and so on

2. Pick up enough bus or train schedules at your local depot for the class to share in groups of two or three. Explain the various arrival and departure columns. Once the students understand the basic layout of these schedules, have them plan a trip. The students should decide the purpose of their trips (shopping, visiting friends, attending a special event, etc.). They should decide how much time they will need to accomplish their purpose, how much money they will need, and if the schedule can accommodate their purposes. Then have each student write a journal entry about his or her imaginary trip. Make sure the students include times and events in these journals.

3. Present your students with a variety of tables and graphs that are missing a key element, such as the title, the key, the intervals on the x or y axis, or a certain measurement within the graph. Have your students supply the missing element.

4. Using tables and graphs as a part of your regular classroom routine will impress your students with the efficiency and practical use of these items. Examples are rosters, calendars listing important school and class events and deadlines, daily schedules and routines, charts that illustrate individual academic achievements such as number of books read, time lines illustrating a current social studies unit, and so on.

5. Have your students locate tables and graphs from various sources: newspapers (*U.S.A. Today* is an excellent resource), magazines, textbooks, atlases. Have each student make a three minute oral presentation based on the information that the table or graph illustrates.

6. When you have your students present oral or written information in content areas, encourage them to incorporate tables and graphs.

7. Students often learn the efficiency of tables and graphs when they make the discovery of how these items can be of personal use. Some ways you can encourage this discovery are the following:

    a. Have students chart their own progress in a certain area that is important to them. Students can chart behavioral items (number of compliments I gave to friends today) as well as academic (number of pages read) and personal items (number of baskets made).

    b. Create a chart notebook where throughout the year students can contribute different types of tables and graphs that they find interesting. Provide blank forms for tables, bar graphs, and coordinate graphs so they can readily fill in numbers and plot points or color the appropriate quantities and labels.

    c. Have the students create and conduct their own personal opinion polls. Then have them illustrate the results of these polls in a table or a graph. This is especially valuable when the students analyze current trends such as fashions, lists of favorites, election choices, and so on.

8. Create a table and a graph that present the same information. Omit certain data on each, and have the students use the alternate source to complete the information for the other.

9. A board game called *Battleship is* widely available in the public domain. This game has the student looking for target coordinates on a grid. The student has to giess which direction on the grid to go to "destroy" an unseen enemy battleship.

10. For fun and practice plotting coordinates, have your students make pictures on dittoed grids by connecting points. Once they get good at this, they can create pictures of their own for their classmates to figure out. The best pictures can be made by presenting the coordinates in series, such as the rocket ship below.

    connect: (5,6), (6,8), (7,6), and (5,6)
    connect: (5,6), (2,3), (5,3), and (5,6)
    connect: (7,6), (10,3), (7,3), and (7,6)
    connect: (7,3), (7,1), (5,1), and (5,3)

11. Two students can play a dice game where the black die represents the x-axis and the white die represents the y-axis. The students roll the dice to plot points on their own grids. The goal can be to create a certain shape, a straight line, and so on. Polyhedra dice can be used to increase the complexity of the grid beyond six by six.

12. A good resource for showing your students how to take opinion polls and turn them into comprehensive graphs and charts is *Mathematics Projects* by Phil Schlemmer (Prentice Hall, 1996).

13. Get maps of large cities, college campuses, towns, museums, and so on that require the observer to find an item or place by using double coordinates. Have your students draw a map of their school or hometown using double coordinates and then correctly place landmarks within the double coordinate system.

14. For a challenge in graph making and collecting data, use *Super Graphs, Venns, and Glyphs* by Honi Bamberger and Patricia Hughs (Scholastic Inc., 1995).

15. Try to develop ways that graphs can be a visual aid for other study skills. For instance, when you are discussing planning study time, a bar graph can be helpful. The students can plot out how many hours of study is required for each course in a week's worth of time.

16. Have your students plot out mathematical equations on a line graph as a way to solve word problems. For instance, the following word problem can be solved by the use of the graph on the next page.

Sue started the bicycle trail at 12:00 P.M., riding 9 kilometers per hour. Martin started one hour later, riding 15 kilometers per hour. About when will Martin overtake Sue?

First make a table for each bicycle showing the distance traveled hour by hour.

Sue

Time	Distance (kilometers)
12:00	0
1:00	9
2:00	18
3:00	27

Martin

Time	Distance (kilometers)
1:00	0
2:00	15
3:00	30

Then plot both bicycles on a line graph. The two lines will cross on the spot where Martin overtakes Sue.

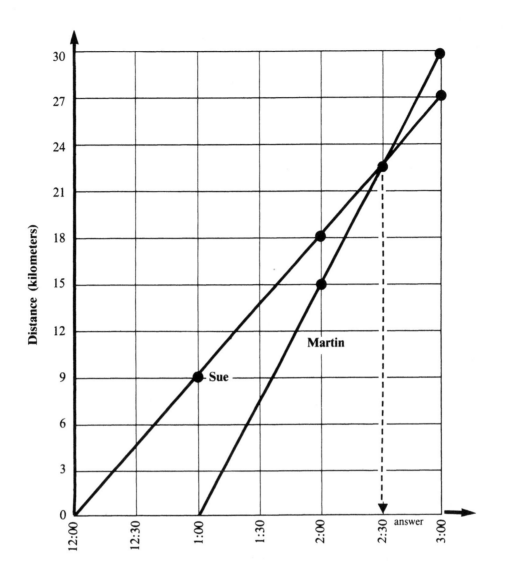

Time

Answer: approximately 2:30

UNIT XIII: USING A DICTIONARY

The dictionary is an essential tool for vocabulary acquisition. Yet students often disregard this tool because they lack the skills for its effective use. They often avoid acquiring these skills because they perceive them as difficult and tedious. Your awareness of your students' reticence may help to minimize their resistance to learning about the uses of the dictionary.

Before you have your students do this unit, we suggest that you examine the dictionary skills that they already have. For this unit to be effective, your students must possess at least some proficiency in the following skills:

1. Basic alphabetizing skills
2. Use of phonetic keys
3. Recognition of the abbreviation of parts of speech
4. Use of guide words
5. Recognition of what a dictionary entry is
6. Ability to choose a definition to match context

The *Challenge* on page 139 is a pretest of your students' awareness of these skills. You will need to have a class set of dictionaries for this exercise.

If your students need work with these skills, you may want to focus on them over a period of several weeks. At the beginning of each class, you can work with one aspect of dictionary use for several minutes. For example, you might say:

"I will give you five minutes to find the page numbers for the following words. See how many you can find!"

"Find two meanings where the word *pick* is used as a noun."

"You have five minutes to find the guide words for the following words..."

"How many dictionary entries are there for the word *up*?"

It's important to correct these exercises immediately and discuss the sources of errors.

Such dictionary skill exercises are also helpful in the building of listening and direction-following skills. You'll find other exercises of this kind in the *Additional Suggestions* for this unit.

SUGGESTED DIRECTIONS FOR UNIT XIII

PLEASE NOTE: To do the *Challenge* on page 139, you need to have a class set of dictionaries. The answers have not been provided for you because they will vary from dictionary to dictionary. You will want to find the answers before this class, so you can provide your students with immediate feedback.

Be sure you have your students do the *Challenge* at least a day before doing the rest of this unit.

DAY 1

1. Pass out the dictionaries. Students can work in pairs if necessary, but it is essential that the students all have the same dictionary.

2. Read over the *Challenge* (page 139) with your students. Then give the following directions. Pause between directions to give your students time to work. Be careful not to repeat yourself.

    "I am going to give you a set of directions. I will say the directions only once. You must listen and follow them.

    "Find the spaces for WORD #1.

    Number 1:   Spell the word *card* in the spaces provided.

    Number 2:   Look up the word. Write the guide words for the word *card* on the line provided.

    Number 3:   How many entries does the word *card* have? Write this number on the line provided.

    Number 4:   Look at entry number #3. Write down what part of speech entry #3 is on the line provided.

    Number 5:   Look at the sentence. Which entry and definition best fit the way *card* is used in this sentence? Write down your answers in the spaces provided.

UNIT XIII: USING A DICTIONARY

CHALLENGE!

The dictionary was probably the first reference book that you became familiar with. You already know a lot about using it. The challenge that your teacher is going to read to you will show you how quickly you can locate and use information from the dictionary.

WORD # 1

1. _ _ _ _

2. _____

3. _____

4. _____

5. After dinner tonight, do you want to play *cards*?

    entry _____ definition _____

WORD # 2

1. _ _ _ _ _

2. _____

3. _____

4. _____

5. Please put the ads at eye *level* so everyone who comes into the store can see them.

    entry _____ definition _____

WORD # 3

1. _ _ _ _

2. _____

3. _____

4. _____

5. If you don't *hush* up, the whole town will know your secret.

    entry _____ definition _____

139

"Find the spaces for WORD #2.

Number 1: Spell the word *level* in the spaces provided.

Number 2: Look up the word. Write the guide words for the word *level* on the line provided.

Number 3: How many entries does the word *level* have? Write this number on the line provided.

238

Number 4: Look at entry number #1. Write down what part of speech entry #1 is on the line provided.

Number 5: Look at the sentence. Which entry and definition best fit the way *level* is used in this sentence? Write down your answers in the spaces provided.

"Find the spaces for WORD #3.

Number 1: Spell the word *hush* in the spaces provided.

Number 2: Look up the word. Write the guide words for the word *hush* on the line provided.

Number 3: How many entries does the word *hush* have? Write this number on the line provided.

Number 4: Look at entry number #2. Write down what part of speech entry #2 is on the line provided.

Number 5: Look at the sentence. Which entry and definition best fit the way *hush* is used in this sentence? Write down your answers in the spaces provided."

Approximate time: 10-15 minutes

THE DICTIONARY - A COMPLICATED RESOURCE

If you had any trouble with the *Challenge*, don't feel bad. This unit will help you to learn more about how to use a dictionary.

EXERCISE I

Directions: Read sentence #1 below. If what the sentence says is true for you, put a check in the space before the sentence. Do the same for sentences #2-4.

Then answer question #5.

1. _____ I have trouble locating words that I don't know how to spell.

2. _____ I do not use guide words to help locate information.

3. _____ I have difficulty choosing the meaning that fits the context of the sentence.

4. _____ I have difficulty figuring out how a word is pronounced.

5.   List any other problems you might have when using a dictionary.

_____

_____

_____

_____

_____

INTRODUCTION

You may have discovered that using a dictionary can be a frustrating experience. You want to learn about the meaning of a word, so you look it up in the dictionary. But, instead of finding one meaning, you find many different ones! What do you do then?

This unit will help you learn how a dictionary is organized and how you can make better use of it.

140

3.   Read aloud *The Dictionary - A Complicated Resource* (page 140) to your students. Have your students do Exercise I (page 140). You will want to examine their answers before going any further with this unit.

10 minutes

DAY 2

1. Find the answers for Exercises II and III (pages 141-143) in your class dictionary. List these answers in your program.

2. At the beginning of the class, divide your students into small groups of two to four members. Equip each student with a dictionary. It is helpful for all students to have the same edition, but this is not essential. (If you don't have enough dictionaries for each student to have one, give each group as many as possible to share.)

3. Read the *Introduction* (page 140) aloud to your students, or have students read it aloud. Read aloud the first section of the directions for Exercise II (pages 141-142), and ask your students to answer this question. Go over the answer. If students reach different answers, briefly discuss how this happened.

10 minutes

EXERCISE II

Directions: Look up the word *run* in your dictionary. Read through its many meanings. How many different meanings are listed for the word *run*? Write the number of different meanings in the blank below.

_____

Read the following sentences carefully. Find the best definition for the word *run* as it is used in each sentence below. Write the correct definition on the line under each sentence.

EXAMPLE

"*Run* and call the vet," she ordered. "I can't seem to give her the help she needs with the colt."

_____

1. "I can *run* faster than you." he snarled at me from the starting gate.

_____

2. She had a *run* in her tights.

_____

3. The dog was not used to his collar and chain. He used to have the *run* of the whole neighborhood.

_____

4. She decided to *run* for Attorney General even though a woman had never held that office before.

_____

5. Even with the critics' praise, the play only had a three month *run* on Broadway.

_____

6. We wait eagerly for the salmon to *run* each year.

_____

Continued on page 142.

141

4. Read the second part of the directions for Exercise II aloud. Go over the *Example* with the class. Then have your students work through this Exercise either individually or in pairs. When they have completed the exercise, go over it orally.

10-15 minutes

7. His fingers seemed to fly over the clarinet as he played the *runs* in the sonata with ease.

   _____

8. He always liked the Phoenix to Los Angeles *run* with its long stretches of open road.

   _____

9. The motorcycle was *run* off the road by a truck.

   _____

10. The ship's captain wanted to *run* the blockade, but the admiral overruled his command.

    _____

EXERCISE III

Directions: The dictionary lists the meanings of a given word. The dictionary also provides other helpful information about words and how to use them.

On page 143 you can see three dictionary entries for the word *trace*. Some parts of these entries are already named. Look over these parts and their names carefully.

Then on the lines provided, name as many of the other numbered parts as you can. Even if you don't know what a part is called, describe what you think the part is or what it does in the dictionary definition.

5. Read the directions for Exercise III (pages 142-143) aloud. Emphasize that students should try to put an answer in each blank, even if they don't know the correct name for some part of the entry. Have your students do this exercise either in small groups or in pairs. When your students have completed the exercise, go over it orally. Discuss and clarify.

   10-15 minutes

1. _____ entry word _____

2. _____

trace¹ / tras / n. **1.** a sign, such as a mark, footprint, track, etc., showing that something has passed by or happened: We found traces of the migrating herds. The outlaws left traces of their overnight camp.

3. _____

4. _____

2. hint or slight evidence: a trace of sorrow. **3.** small amount: There was a trace of mercury found in the tuna. **4.** in psychology, the changing of brain cells set up by repeated events considered to be the physiological foundation of memory. **5.** a mark or some such sign made by an instrument which records: The polygraph trace is designed to show the intensity of the subject's response.

5. _____

6. _____

trace² / tras / vb. **1.** to sketch over, drawing by placing a transparent piece of paper over a map, drawing or photo. **2.** to draw with care, i.e., figures or lines. **3.** to review in outline form: We traced the development of the Incas. **4.** to be guided by marks or signs: The hunters traced the wounded deer by following her blood stains. **5.** to show a record of: The polygraph traced the subject's responses. **traced, tracing.** (from Old French tracier, from Latin tractus, from trahere, "to draw")

7. _____

8. _____

trace³ / tras / n. **1.** either of two straps attached to the animal and a vehicle which is drawn by the animal **2.** LEADER **3.** one or more vascular bundles supplying a leaf or twig. **4.** connecting bar or rod pivoted at each end to another piece to transmit motion from (Old French meaning "traces" from Latin tractus, "a dragging") **kick over the traces** Informal showing independence or insubordination

9. _____

10. Idiom — found in dark print after the entry. _____

143

EXERCISE IV

Directions: Using the dictionary entries on page 143, write the best meaning for the way *trace* is used in each of the following sentences on the line below each sentence.

EXAMPLE

There are *traces* of arsenic in the dead man's body.

_____

1. He carefully *traced* the treasure map onto the see-through paper.

   _____

2. We found no *traces* of the lost pony.

   _____

3. She looked at the old homestead with a *trace* of regret in her eyes.

   _____

4. The *trace* from the stem to the leaf carries nitrogen that is needed for photosynthesis.

   _____

5. We *traced* the bear tracks to the stream.

   _____

6. The lesson was designed to *trace* the rise and the fall of the Roman Empire.

   _____

7. She examined the graph that the machine had drawn by measuring his heart beat. The *traces* showed possible signs of heart weakness.

   _____

8. The *traces* snapped, and the frightened horse ran off as the wagon rolled to a bumpy halt.

   _____

9. She *traced* her ancestry back to the first Dutch settlers.

   _____

10. A tiny *trace* in the watch had broken, stopping the movement of the hour hand.

    _____

144

6. Exercise IV (page 144) can be used as further classwork or as homework.

UNIT XIII SUMMARY: USING A DICTIONARY

One word can have many different meanings. You can use the dictionary to learn about the various meanings of a word and to figure out which meanings you need to learn.

The dictionary can also give you other helpful information about a word:

1. how the word is pronounced;
2. the part or parts of speech of the word;
3. examples of how the word can be used;
4. various forms of the word: for example, plural, past tense, and so on; and
5. any special uses of the word.

ANSWERS FOR EXERCISES IN UNIT XIII

Pages 141-142: Exercise II

Number of meanings listed for *run:* depends on your dictionary.

Accept any reasonable answer in this exercise.

Example: to go rapidly or hurriedly

1. to go faster than a walk
2. a ravel in a knitted fabric
3. freedom of movement
4. enter into an election
5. an unbroken course of performances
6. to go up river to spawn
7. a rapid scale or passage
8. a route traveled with regularity
9. forced or pushed
10. slip through or breakthrough

Pages 142-143: Exercise III

Accept any reasonable answers.

2. shows how a word is pronounced
3. the seond meaning of the first entry
4. using the meaning in a sentence as an example
5. shows that this is the second entry for the word
6. part of speech
7. inflected forms, or verb endings
8. part of speech
9. derivation, or what language the word comes from

Page 144: Exercise IV

Example: small amount

1. drawing by placing a transparent piece of paper over a map
2. a sign that something has passed by
3. hint or slight evidence
4. one or more of the vascular bundles supplying a leaf or twig
5. to be guided by marks or signs
6. to review in outline form
7. a mark or sign made by an instrument that records
8. either of two straps attached to an animal and to the vehicle that is drawn by the animal
9. to be guided by marks or signs
10. connecting bar or rod

ADDITIONAL SUGGESTIONS

1. Use an imaginary word exercise like the one described in the *Additional Suggestions* for Unit XII. Or have your students make up their own imaginary words. Then ask them to create dictionary entries for their imaginary words and use the words in sentences.

2. Have your students make up imaginary words and write them phonetically, using a dictionary pronounciation key. They can exchange words with a partner and take turns pronouncing the imaginary words.

3. Explore homographs like these:

ob ject′	ob′ ject
rec′ ord	re′ cord
con′ sole	con sole′

    Help your students to discover that such words have not only different pronounciations and different meanings, but they also are different parts of speech.

4. Have a dictionary word a day. Select words that have prefixes and the possibility of adding suffixes. Play with the word by adding the suffixes and discussing how suffix variations affect both meaning and part of speech. Offer the word in different contexts to show nuances in meaning. You might want to have the students make colorful illustrations showing how the same word can have many different applications.

5. Play the dictionary game in small groups. For this game you need an intermediate dictionary and several small slips of paper for each group.

6. One student, the *leader,* finds an obscure or unusual word in the dictionary. She or he announces the word to the group and writes the meaning of the word on a slip of paper. All of the students in the group make up a definition for the word and write their definitions on a slip of paper. The *leader* collects the slips, includes the one with the correct definition, and shuffles them. The *leader* then reads aloud all of the definitions. The other students in the group vote for which defintion they believe to be the correct one. The *leader* then tells the group which definition is correct.

    For the next word, another student acts as the *leader.*

    Each student earns a point for each vote her or his definition earns. The *leader* earns a point for each incorrect vote.

    Note that the game described above is available commercially as Balderdash, by Parker Brothers.

UNIT XIV: PUTTING A BOOK TOGETHER

This unit is designed to help your students gain an understanding of the various parts of a standard textbook and what their uses are. Most students in the middle school years do not view their texts as sources or references. While they may have some awareness of the various parts of a text, like the glossary or the index, they tend not to use these sections of their books in an effective way.

This unit will involve your students in creating examples of the various parts of a text other than the body of the book. These activities can help your students to understand clearly the structure of a textbook and to begin to view their texts as tools that they can use for their own learning.

If your students are not at all familiar with the parts of a textbook addressed in this unit (title page, copyright page, table of contents, body or text, glossary, index, bibliography), you may want to introduce them to your students in a gradual way and employ the descriptions of these parts included in this unit as a review. For example, you could spend a few minutes at the beginning of class over a week or two teaching your students about these parts of a textbook.

SUGGESTED DIRECTIONS FOR UNIT XIV

We suggest that this unit be worked as a whole class project. It will require approximately two periods of class time.

Your students will be engaged in creating, sharing, and using parts of a "textbook." As you examine this unit, consider how you would prefer to have your students share the parts of the "textbook" that they create. Keep in mind that what your students create on the first day will be shared and used on the second day.

You may want to use one of the following methods:

a. Have your students write on large pieces of newsprint or a substitute that can be hung up in the front of the room.

b. Have your students write on the board if your classroom has sufficient board space.

c. Have your students write on ditto masters with which you can make copies after the first day of the unit.

UNIT XIV: PUTTING A BOOK TOGETHER

INTRODUCTION

Almost every textbook has many different parts other than just the *body* or *text* of the book, that is, the written sections in each chapter. Most of your textbooks have all of the parts listed below:

> Title page, and copyright page
> Table of Contents
> Body or text
> Glossary
> Index
> Bibliography

When you know how to find and use all of these parts, your textbook can become more helpful to you in your learning.

In this unit, you'll learn about the different parts of a textbook by putting a book together. The *body* of the "book" you will put together is actually an article called "Monkey Business."

EXERCISE I

Directions: Turn to page 151, and *survey* the article "Monkey Business."

TITLE PAGE AND COPYRIGHT PAGE

The *title page* is the very beginning of a book. The *title page* tells you the title of the book. It also lists the author and publisher and where the book was published.

The *copyright page* is usually right after the title page. This page tells you who has the right to print the book and when the book was first printed.

146

DAY 1

1. Read the *Introduction* (page 146) aloud to your students. Discuss briefly. Then have your students do Exercise I (page 146); give them three minutes to conduct their surveys.

    Approximate time: 5-8 minutes

2. Have a student or students read *Title Page And Copyright Page* (page 146) aloud. Then do Exercise II (page 147) as a class. Do parts A and B orally; write part C on the board or on newsprint. (If you are using dittoes, be sure to copy the title and copyright pages from the board onto a master, and make copies available to your students for the second day of this unit.)

    5-10 minutes

EXERCISE II

Directions: (A) Find the *title page* in this study skills *Program*, and locate the following information:

What is the title of this book?

Who is the author?

Who published the book?

Where was the book published?

(B) Find the *copyright page* of this book. Locate the following information:

Who has the right to print this book?

When was this book first printed?

(C) Using the title page and copyright page in this book as a source of information and as a model, make up a *title page* for *Monkey Business*.

TABLE OF CONTENTS

The *table of contents* tells you what you will find inside the book. It lets you know about the main ideas that are covered in the book. The *table of contents* also tells you how many chapters there are in the book and on what page each chapter begins.

You can find the *table of contents* in the front of the book, usually right after the copyright page.

EXERCISE III

Directions: (A) Find the *table of contents* in this study skills *Program*, and examine it.

(B) Read over the "book" *Monkey Business*. Decide what the chapter headings should be, and make a list of these headings.

(C) Create a *table of contents* for *Monkey Business*. Your table of contents should contain chapter titles and pages on which the chapters begin.

3. If your students could benefit from a review of the table of contents, the glossary, the index, and the bibliography, read aloud the descriptive sections about these textbook parts (pages 147-150), or have students read them aloud. Discuss briefly. (This step can be omitted if your students already have sufficient awareness of these textbook parts.)

5-8 minutes

4. Divide your class into work groups as follows:

   a. Have about 20% of your students do Exercise III (page 147) *and* Exercise VI (page 150).

   b. Have about 40% of your students do Exercise IV (page 148).

   c. Have about 40% of your students do Exercise V (page 149).

If you omitted direction #3 above, tell your students to read the descriptions above their assigned exercises carefully before they begin work.

Have your students work on the assigned exercises. Tell them to follow the directions carefully. Also, give them the necessary materials for creating their group products, i.e. newsprint and magic markers, or chalk and board space, or ditto masters. Provide them with whatever instruction they need to make a product that can be easily shared.

You will probably want to circulate among the groups and help them get started. You may also want to help them with the task of dividing the work within their exercises.

20-30 minutes

5. Collect the finished group products at the end of the period.

GLOSSARY

The *glossary* of a textbook is a lot like a dictionary for that book. It lists words that are new or unfamiliar to most readers and tells you how the words are pronounced, what part of speech they are, and what their meanings are.

The *glossary* covers meanings that are used within that book. It often doesn't list every meaning of a word as a dictionary would.

You can usually find the *glossary* at the end of the body of the book.

EXERCISE IV

Directions: (A) Read the "book" *Monkey Business*.

(B) There are 17 underlined words or terms in the body of *Monkey Business*. Find all of these words or terms; make a list of them, and put the list into alphabetical order.

PLEASE NOTE! A term is a group of words that have a particular meaning together. The terms in *Monkey Business* are animal behaviorists, endangered species, and hurdy-gurdy man.

In a *glossary*, terms like these are listed as if they were a single word.

(C) Using context clues or a dictionary, write a glossary definition for each underlined word or term in the body of the "book." Be sure to use the same meaning that is used in *Monkey Business*.

(D) Put your words and definitions together, so you have a *glossary* for *Monkey Business*.

148

254

INDEX

An *index* lists specific names and ideas found within a book. This list is in alphabetical order. Numbers of the pages where ideas and names can be found are listed after the names and ideas.

You can usually find the *index* at the very back of the book. Some reference books have a separate volume for the index.

EXERCISE V

Directions: (A) All of the words and terms in the list below appear in the "book" *Monkey Business.* Put this list of words and terms into alphabetical order.

Pre-monkey	Tree shrew	Bushbaby
Tarsier	New World monkeys	Old World monkeys
Proboscis monkey	Spider monkey	Hurdy-gurdy man
Monkeys as pets	Zoos	Endangered species
Colobus monkey	Guenons	Woolly monkey
Howler monkey	Uakari	Langur
Macaque	Owl monkey	Marmoset
Mangabeys		

       (B) Read the "book" *Monkey Business.* As you read, locate the words from the list above in the body of the book. Each time that you find a word in the body of the book, write that page number after the word in the list.

           Make sure you find each time that each word appears.

       (C) Put all of the words and page numbers together, so you have an index for *Monkey Business.*

149

BIBLIOGRAPHY

A *bibliography* is a list of references that an author has used to help him or her write a book or article. References can include books or articles.

A *bibliography* lists the references alphabetically by the author's last name.

A *bibliography* is set up in the following way:

> Author's last name, First name. *Title*. Place published: Name of publisher, Date published.

You can usually find the *bibliography* just before the index at the back of the book.

EXERCISE VI

Directions: (A) Arrange the references for *Monkey Business* listed below in correct alphabetical order.

(B) Write out a *bibliography* for *Monkey Business*. Be sure that you have punctuated everything correctly.

Whitlock, Ralph, *Chimpanzees*. Milwaukee: Raintree Children's Books, 1977.

Morris, Dean. *Monkeys and Apes*. Milwaukee: Raintree Children's Books, 1977.

Shuttlesworth, Dorothy. *Monkeys, Great Apes, and Small Apes*. Garden City, New York: Doubleday and Company, Inc., 1972.

Leen, Nina. *Monkeys*. New York: Holt, Rinehart, and Winston, 1976.

Annixter, Jane and Paul. *Monkeys and Apes*. New York: Franklin Watts, 1976.

150

256

MONKEY BUSINESS

Introduction: A Brief History

At zoos, people often find themselves standing in front of monkey cages. They stare at the intelligent animals that seem curiously like humans. Monkeys can use simple tools, and their hands twist and turn cleverly. Monkeys even seem to have emotions. Actually, monkeys are like humans in another way. They both belong to the same group of *mammals*, as do chimpanzees and apes. This group is called *primates*. All primates have grasping hands or feet, well-developed vision, and relatively large brains.

tree shrew

The primate story began many millions of years ago. A "pre-monkey" known as the *tree shrew* made its appearance on the earth about 70 million years ago. It preferred the high tree tops where it could look down safely upon the giants we know as dinosaurs. It was one of the first mammals. Since it was so tiny, the *tree shrew* was timid. It preferred hiding to fighting. Its clever, long fingers, a brain that was large for its size, and its ability in climbing made the tree shrew a survivor. It still lives today, long after the dinosaurs, on the island of Madagascar (a large island off the eastern coast of Africa).

The tree shrew, the *bushbaby*, and the *tarsier* are some of the animals we call "pre-monkeys." They are like monkeys in many ways, but they aren't as highly developed as monkeys are.

tarsier

Notice the huge, staring eyes. Unlike "real" monkey's eyes, these eyes cannot move within their sockets.

bushbaby

The first of the "real" monkeys emerged about 30 million years ago. Unlike the "pre-monkey," monkeys have eyes that move in their sockets, arms and legs more useful for speedy climbing and running, hands better developed for holding, and a larger and more complicated brain.

Continued on page 152.

151

Two Classifications

Monkeys come in all sizes, shapes, and colors. But they fit into two large *classifications* or categories These classifications are Old World monkeys and New World monkeys. They are put into these classifications because of where they are found. Old World monkeys are found in the rain forests of Africa and Asia. They are also found in the islands off these *continents*. New World monkeys are found in the rain forests of South America and Central America. A few can even be found in Mexico There are many noticeable differences between these two kinds of monkeys

Old World Monkeys

Old World monkeys are generally considered to have more intelligence than New World monkeys. They will often use simple tools, such as a stick for digging out delicious ants or a rock for killing small game. Their noses are more like human noses than those of New World monkeys are. They are narrow and point downward.

Old World monkeys have 32 teeth, the same as humans have. They have tough protective pads under their *haunches*.

At one time, *animal behaviorists*, scientists who study animal behavior, thought that Old World monkeys were more disagreeable than New World monkeys, Old World monkeys were believed to be more dangerous as they fiercely guarded their *territories*. Modern animal behaviorists disagree. They point to the poor conditions under which the first studies were made. The monkeys were kept in small cages, were not fed proper foods, and often were teased. No wonder the monkeys appeared to be fierce!

New World Monkeys

New World monkeys often have a long and agile tail; most Old World monkeys do not. This tail can be used as another hand for grasping and swinging. These tails are called *prehensile* because of their grasping qualities.

The New World monkeys have broad and round noses. They rely on *instinct* for survival. They rarely use tools as Old World monkeys do. Their bodies are generally longer and slimmer. This makes climbing and traveling through the trees easier. Almost all New World monkeys live in trees. Some Old World monkeys get too heavy to feel comfortable staying high up in the air on slender branches.

Proboscis Monkey

Proboscis means long-nosed in Latin. The bright red head and the long nose of the adult proboscis make it one of the strangest looking creatures in the animal world. The adult male's nose can reach three inches below its chin. Scientists believe this nose could be the sounding board for the long drawn out "honk" or "kee-honk" of the proboscis. The proboscis lives in the rain forests of Borneo, an island in the western Pacific Ocean, and travels through the trees in large, noisy troops.

The proboscis is an example of an Old World monkey. It may weigh less than a pound at birth, but when full grown, the male can weigh up to fifty pounds. The female weighs about twenty-five pounds. The proboscis does not have sunken eyes like many monkeys. Its eyes are small, and it seems to look out intelligently. A baby proboscis' nose will start out looking much like any other monkey's nose. As the monkey matures, the nose grows, and the lips draw into a smile. It's almost as if the proboscis knows what a strange looking character it is!

The proboscis eats large amounts of leaves. It also enjoys shoots from mangoes and other fruit. However, it is not an overworked monkey, constantly on the lookout for food. It eats when it wants to. It usually prefers to spend its time lounging on its back or sitting motionless among the tree leaves. The proboscis also enjoys an occasional swim in a tropical river or lake.

Proboscis monkey
watching from
his tree top.

152

258

Hunters value the proboscis monkey for its rust colored fur. This is one reason why the proboscis is on the *endangered species* list.

Proboscis male- his nose can be three inches longer than his chin!

Spider Monkey

One of the most common New World monkeys is the spider monkey. This monkey gets its name because of its "spider-like" appearance as it moves through the trees at remarkable speeds. Its prehensile or grasping tail helps it to be quick and agile. It uses its tail to climb high into the rain forests of South and Central America and Mexico. The tail can also help the spider monkey grab bits of food as it stretches down from the trees. The end of the tail has a patch of bare skin that is very sensitive. It can pick up a small fruit or a peanut.

The spider monkey usually travels in small bands or groups. However, up to thirty spider monkeys have been seen traveling together. Their voices cut through the rain forest in a high pitched warning yelp. This sounds a lot like many barking terriers.

One of the spider monkey's favorite sports is wrestling. It does not like to swim, even though experiments have shown that it can swim quite well. The spider monkey prefers to hook its long tail on a branch and swing back and forth like a hammock.

The spider monkey is the monkey we picture traveling with the *hurdy-gurdy man*. The traveling musician would play his wind-up organ on the street as his spider monkey begged for coins.

Spider-reaching for delicate bits.

"Hurdy-gurdy" man and his trained monkey.

Continued on page 154.

153

259

Monkeys in Captivity

Monkeys don't usually adapt very well as pets. They seem quite happy and sweet when they are young but often grow up to be moody and unpredictable. They bite and spit at times and do cute tricks at other times.

Zoos keep many types of monkeys. These monkeys adapt very well if they have large, clean cages, which also have equipment for climbing and swinging.

Besides having monkeys for people to watch, zoos want to help any monkeys that are an endangered species. Monkeys are hunted for food, fur, pets, and medical research. Also, each year more and more acres of rain forest are being cut down by farmers and builders. Monkey populations all over the world are on the _decline_. Since monkeys _breed_, or reproduce their young, very well in captivity, a well-kept zoo is an important place for them.

Some information about the kinds of monkeys you might find in a zoo is listed below.

Type of Monkey	Zoo Life Span	Home Continent
Colobus monkey	8-12 years	Africa
Guenons	20-30 years	Africa
Howler monkey	10-15 years	Central, South America
Langur	10-20 years	Asia
Macaque	25-30 years	Asia
Mangabeys	15-20 years	Africa
Marmoset	2-8 years	South America
Owl monkey	10-13 years	Central, South America
Proboscis monkey	4-10 years	Asia
Spider monkey	17-20 years	South, Central America
Uakari	5-9 years	South America
Woolly monkey	10-12 years	South America

Perhaps you'll go to a zoo one day. If you do, stand in front of the monkey cage and try to imagine being in the rain forests of South America, Central America, Africa, or Asia. Don't be surprised if you think you see a monkey look right at you and then seem to be laughing. The monkey may just think humans are strange looking creatures!

154

260

DAY 2

1. Display or hand out the various parts of a "textbook" that your students have created. Have your students do Exercise VII (page 155) individually. Go over the exercise.

   10-15 minutes

EXERCISE VIII

Directions: Answer the questions below, using the parts of the "book" *Monkey Business* that you have put together. Then, in the marked space, write which part(s) of the book you used to help you answer the question.

EXAMPLE

What chapter would you read if you wanted to learn about how monkeys live in zoos?

_____

Part of the book: _____

1. Are you a mammal? Name three kinds of mammals

   _____

   _____

   Part of the book: _____

2. Where does the squirrel monkey live?

   _____

   Part of the book: _____

3. Where are Raintree Children's Books published?

   _____

   Part of the book: _____

4. What kind of question might you ask an animal behaviorist about your pet dog?

   _____

   _____

   Part of the book: _____

156

2.   Read the directions for Exercise VIII (pages 156-157) aloud. Go over the example orally. Then have your students do the exercise. Go over the exercise; discuss for emphasis.

15-20 minutes

5. Are monkeys good pets? Why or why not?

_____

_____

   Part of the book: _____

6. Where would you find a description of the Proboscis monkey?

_____

   Part of the book: _____

UNIT XIV SUMMARY: PUTTING A BOOK TOGETHER

You can use your textbooks better to help you learn when you understand how the parts of a book fit together. Also, when you want to find out specific information, knowing the parts of a textbook and how to use them can save you time and effort.

The main parts of a textbook are these:

1. The *title page* tells you the title of the book. It also tells you the author, the publisher, and where the book was published.

2. The *copyright page* tells you who owns the right to print the book and when the book was first printed.

3. The *table of contents* informs you about what the chapters are in the book and on what page each one starts. It can also help you to find out what main ideas are covered within the book.

4. The *body* or *text* of the book includes all of the written sections in each chapter.

5. The *glossary* is like a dictionary for new or unfamiliar words used in the book. Words in a glossary are listed in alphabetical order; each listing tells you the meaning of that word as it is used in the book.

6. The *index* is an alphabetical listing of specific names and ideas found within a book. Numbers of the pages where the names and ideas can be found are listed after the names and ideas.

7. The *bibliography* lists all of the references, the books and articles that the author has used in writing the book.

157

ANSWERS FOR EXERCISES IN UNIT XIV

Page 147: Exercise II

You can use the specific information from the **hm Study Skills Program: Level I.** Or use the **Program** only as a model and have your students invent information for the copyright and title pages; ask them to use their imagination and sense of humor!

Page 147: Exercise III

TABLE OF CONTENTS

I. Introduction: A Brief History   page #
II. Two Classifications   page #
III. Old World Monkeys   page #
IV. New World Monkeys   page #
V. Proboscis Monkey   page #
VI. Spider Monkey   page #
VII. Monkeys in Captivity   page #

Page 148: Exercise IV

GLOSSARY

animal behaviorist: a scientist who studies animal behavior
breed: produce offspring or young
bushbaby: one kind of "premonkey," has large eyes that cannot move in their sockets
classification: category
continent: one of the grand divisions of land on the Earth, of which there are seven: Asia, Africa, Europe, North America, South America, Australia, Antartica
decline: getting smaller, moving towards extinction
endangered species: a kind of animal whose population has become so small that it is in danger of being wiped out
haunches: hips or hindquarters
hurdy-gurdy man: traveling musician who plays an accordian and has a monkey who begs coins for him
instinct: a kind of behavior in which an animal acts automatically; instincts are not learned but are part of the animal from birth
mammals: a class of animals that have backbones and nourish their young with milk
prehensile: adapted for seizing or grasping
primates: an order of mammals consisting of humans, apes, monkeys, and "premonkeys"
proboscis: a long, flexible snout or nose
tarsier: one kind of "pre-monkey," has large eyes that cannot move in their sockets
territory: an area of land that an animal lives in and will defend against intruders
tree shrew: the first "pre-monkey"

Page 149: Exercise V

INDEX

Bushbaby, p. #
Colobus monkey, p. #
Endangered species, p. #
Guenons, p. #
Howler monkey, p. #
Hurdygurdy man, p. #
Langur, p. #
Macaque, p. #

Mangabeys, p. #
Marmoset, p. #
Monkeys as pets, p. #
New World monkeys, p. #
Old World monkeys, p. #
Owl monkey, p. #
Premonkey, p. #
Proboscis monkey, p. #

Spider monkey, p. #
Tarsier, p. #
Tree shrew, p. #
Uakari, p. #
Woolly monkey, p. #
Zoos, p. #

Page 155: Exercise VII

1. No. There's no mention of what monkeys eat.
2. Answers will vary.
3. The "premonkey's" eyes do not move in their sockets.
4. *Chimpanzees* and *Monkeys and Apes* were both published in 1977.

Pages l56-157: Exercise VIII

Example: Chapter VII; table of contents
1. Yes; answers will vary; glossary
2. South America; index and body
3. Milwaukee; bibliography
4. Answers will vary; glossary
5. No; body
6. Page #; index

ADDITIONAL SUGGESTIONS

1. Good resources about how to "make books" are *A Book of One's Own: Developing Literacy through Making Books* by Paul Johnson (Heineman, 1993) and How to Make Books with Children by JoEileen Moore (Evan-Moore, 1999).

2. Have your students create "book parts" for pieces of their own writing. Select a "book part" that would be a constructive addition to what they have written.

3. Develop worksheets that ask your students to use the various parts of a textbook in involving and challenging ways.

UNIT XV: STUDYING AND TEST TAKING

This unit engages your students in examining their own study environment and behavior. It also introduces your students to a series of skills for answering the most common kinds of objective test questions.

The key to the first part of this unit is that people learn best in their own personal ways. Usually, however, little instruction in school is directed toward the discovery of various aspects of the student's *learning style*. This unit offers the student a way to begin to learn about the characteristics of his or her own learning style by focusing on the student's preferred learning environment. Then the student is encouraged to experiment with the way he or she learns facts.

"Testwiseness" involves understanding the various kinds of questions asked, the kinds of answers they require, and what thinking processes one can use to answer questions most effectively. The second part of this unit is based on the assumption that a student who is "testwise" will be able to show what he or she has learned more effectively. It seems only fair to help students understand how tests work so that they can accurately convey what they know to others.

UNIT XV: STUDYING AND TEST TAKING

INTRODUCTION: STUDYING - FINDING THE RIGHT ENVIRONMENT

Studying means learning. When you are studying to be a musician, a carpenter, or a soccer player, you need the right *environment* for your learning. The *environment* is everything that surrounds you. For example, when you are learning to play a musical instrument, you need a quiet place where you can hear what you're playing and where no one will bother you.

When you are studying for school, you also need the right *study environment*. The first part of this unit will help you to think about what kind of *study environment* is good for you and the way you learn. It will also give you a few suggestions for how you might make better use of your study time.

EXERCISE I

Directions: Read the paragraphs below, and follow the instructions in the third paragraph.

Suzanne's teacher spent the first few days of school talking about the conditions in a good study or learning environment. He said that people have different learning styles and so different people learn best in different kinds of *study environments*. He wanted all of his students to experiment with different *study environments* and find out what helped them to learn better.

Suzanne tried many different conditions before she found the environment that was best for her. Her two most different experiments are pictured on page 159.

Look at the pictures of Suzanne's two study environments. Then, on the lines below, write down all the differences you see.

ENVIRONMENT #1   **ENVIRONMENT #2**

_____   _____
_____   _____
_____   _____
_____   _____
_____   _____
_____   _____
_____   _____

158

SUGGESTED DIRECTIONS FOR UNIT XV

1. Read the *Introduction: Studying* (page 158) aloud, or have your students read it to themselves. Discuss briefly. Then have your students do Exercise I (page 158). (You may want to instruct your students to start Exercise II when they have finished Exercise I).

Approximate time: 10-15 minutes

Environment #1

Environment #2

159

268

EXERCISE II

Directions: Look at both of the lists you've made on page 158. Circle all of the conditions in both lists that would distract or bother *you* if you were trying to learn.

Now make a list on the lines below of what you would want in an environment that would help you study.

_____

_____

_____

_____

_____

_____

TIPS FOR STUDYING

1. Each person seems to have good times of the day for learning. When do you learn best? In the morning, the afternoon, or the evening? Try to figure out when is the best time for you to study.

2. When you study at home, ask your family to help you by keeping things fairly quiet.

3. Get a small notebook to write down what you have to do for homework. Before you leave school, check your notebook. Then ask yourself, "What will I need to take home tonight?" Make sure you take everything you need home with you.

4. Have your materials together when you start to study. Ask yourself, "Do I need a pencil and paper? A dictionary? Anything else?"

5. How long can you pay attention when you're doing your school work? Experiment to find out. If you can concentrate for fifteen or twenty minutes, plan to study for that long. Then do something active and fun for a few minutes before you start again.

6. Each time that you plan to study, set goals for yourself. These goals should be things that you can really do in the time you have. For example, you may not be able to read an entire book for a book report. Instead, decide how many chapters you can read, and try to reach your goal.

160

2. Have your students do Exercise II (page 160). When your students have finished Exercise II, discuss their ideas for a good study environment. (You may also want to discuss Exercise I at this time.) Have several students write their lists on the board, and discuss. Or have your students discuss their lists in small groups. Find out which characteristics of a good study environment are most generally accepted by your students, and list these on the board. Perhaps a few students could design a poster about study environment using the ideas that the class has generated.

10-20 minutes

3. Have students read the *Tips For Studying* (page 160) aloud. Briefly discuss each one.

5-8 minutes

WHAT IS YOUR LEARNING STYLE?

In the *Introduction to Learning and Study Skills you* thought about your learning style, or the way you learn best. Some people learn best when they *hear* information. Others learn best by *writing* important details. Sometimes *picturing the facts* is a good way to learn. Another way to learn is to *try to connect* or make sense of how facts fit together. Most of us learn by combining these ways.

When you pay attention to how you learn best, you will be able to learn more effectively.

EXPERIMENT WITH YOUR LEARNING STYLE

EXERCISE III: PART A

Directions: You will experiment to see how you learn the best. Look at the chart called *Facts About the First Five American Presidents* on page 162. You will have five minutes to try to memorize the facts. Then you will be asked to fill in the blanks on a similar chart.

Think about ways that you learn the best. Try some of the following ways:

1. Say the facts aloud to yourself.

2. Study the lists. Then cover the lists and see if you can remember the information.

3. Write the facts on another piece of paper.

4. Think of the facts in a way that makes sense to you. For example: Of the first five American presidents, three of them were Democratic-Republican. Each of the first five presidents, except for John Adams, had eight years in office. James Monroe was famous for the Monroe Doctrine.

161

4. Read *What Is Your Learning Style?* (page 161) aloud. Discuss briefly.

5. Read the directions for Exercise III: Part A (page 161) aloud, or have a student read them aloud. Discuss the directions and the techniques. Stress that students should experiment with techniques rather than take an actual test. Then have your students do the exercise.

8-10 minutes

FACTS ABOUT THE FIRST FIVE AMERICAN PRESIDENTS

NAME	WHEN ELECTED	PARTY	FAMOUS FOR
George Washington	1789	None	First President
			General in revolution
John Adams	1797	Federalist	Helped write the Declaration of Independence
			First President to live in Washington
Thomas Jefferson	1801	Democratic-Republican	Author of Declaration of Independence
			Scientist farmer
			Architect
James Madison	1809	Democratic-Republican	Founder of the Constitution
			Husband of Dolly
			Wrote 9 Amendments
James Monroe	1817	Democratic-Republican	Hero of the Revolution
			Monroe Doctrine

Directions: Now see how many facts you remember. Fill in the blank spaces below. When you have finished, turn back to the previous chart and check your answers.

REMEMBER: This is an experiment to see how you learn; this is not a test. It is more important to recognize how you learn than to pay attention to how many facts you remember.

FACTS ABOUT THE FIRST FIVE AMERICAN PRESIDENTS

NAME	WHEN ELECTED	PARTY	FAMOUS FOR
1. _____	1789	None	First President
			2. _____
			_____
John Adams	3. _____	Federalist	4. Helped write the
			_____
			_____
			First President to live in Washington
5. _____	1801	Democratic-Republican	Author of Declaration of Independence
			6. _____
			Architect
James Madison	7. _____	8. _____	9. Founder of the
			_____
			10. Husband of _____
			11. Wrote _____ Amendments
12. _____	1817	Democratic-Republican	13. Hero of the _____
			14. _____ Doctrine

163

6. After five minutes have elapsed, read aloud the directions for Exercise III: Part B (page 163). Then have your students do this exercise. When they have completed the exercise, have them do Exercise IV (page 164). Then engage them in discussing their responses to the exercise. Point out differences in *learning styles,* and encourage your students to become more aware of their own styles of learning.

10 minutes

EXERCISE IV

Directions: Look at the statements below. Check the statements that apply to you.

_____ 1. I learn facts best by writing them.
_____ 2. I learn facts best when I see them in lists and memorize what the lists look like.
_____ 3. I learn facts best when I say them aloud.
_____ 4. I learn facts best by combining #1 - #3.
_____ 5. I have a difficult time memorizing facts, but I can remember facts when I see how they all fit together.

INTRODUCTION: TEST TAKING

When you put your time and effort into studying for a test, you want to do well. To do that, you need to learn the material that the test covers. You can also do better on tests if you understand how to answer the different kinds of questions. This part of the unit will suggest some tips you can use with five different types of questions:

> true/false questions
> matching questions
> multiple choice questions
> short answer questions
> fact/opinion questions

164

7. Read the *Introduction: Test Taking* (page 164) aloud, or have a student read it aloud. Discuss briefly. Then read and discuss the material under the heading *True/False Questions* (page 165). Read the directions for Exercise V (page 165) aloud, or have a student read them aloud. Have the students do this exercise. Correct and discuss briefly.

<u>5-10 minutes</u>

273

TRUE/FALSE QUESTIONS

True/false questions are statements that you are asked to judge: are they true or false?

Tips for true/false questions

1. Read the question carefully. If *any part* of the statement is false, then it is a false statement. Mark it false.

2. Watch for "key words" like the ones listed below. Think about what these words mean in the statement; they can help you make a decision.

always	all	never
only	usually	often
frequently		

EXERCISE V

Directions: Read the statements below. Decide whether each statement is true or false. Mark a T for true or an F for false in the space before each statement.

_____ 1. All people who live in Norway have blond hair.

_____ 2. Mercury, Venus, Jupiter, Mars, and the Earth's moon are planets within our solar system.

_____ 3. All even numbers can be divided evenly by two.

_____ 4. Plants never grow unless they get direct sunlight.

_____ 5. A calm always comes before a thunderstorm.

_____ 6. Animals usually have their young in the spring.

165

8. Follow the same procedure of reading the headings, reading the directions, and doing the exercises for Exercises VI-IX. You may choose to have your students work through these exercises individually, or you may want to work as a class. Correct the exercises together when your students have finished. Discuss any questions that they might have.

When you are discussing facts and opinions, be sure to stress that opinions are not wrong, but to be valid they must be based on facts. Facts, however, can be wrong.

15-30 minutes

SHORT ANSWER QUESTIONS

Short answer questions ask you to write in the correct answer as part of a statement. They are also called "fill in the blank" questions.

Tips for short answer questions

1. Read the question carefully. Ask yourself: what is this question asking? Then write in the answer if you know it.

2. If you don't know the exact answer but do know something that is related to it, write down what you *do* know. You may get partial credit for it.

3. If you don't know the correct answer but have an idea about it, make a good guess!

EXERCISE VII

Directions: Read the statements below. Fill in the best answer that you know.

1. There are _____ months of the year that begin with the letter "J".

2. The sixth American president was _____ .

3. The three states of matter are gas, solid, and _____ .

4. The author of *The Chronicles of Narnia* is _____ .

5. The United States is bordered by two other countries. The northern border country is

_____ . The southern border country is _____ .

MATCHING QUESTIONS

Matching questions usually give you two lists of information and ask you to match things on one list with things on the other.

Tips for matching questions

1. Match the easiest things first, the ones you know most about.

2. When you've matched an item, cross out its number or letter, so you know you've already done it.

3. If you're not sure about any of the items, make a good guess!

EXERCISE VIII

Directions: Read the two lists below. Write the number of the piece of sports equipment in the blank before the sport for which you'd use the equipment.

a. _____ baseball   1. shoulder pads

b. _____ football   2. hoop

c. _____ basketball   3. foil

d. _____ field hockey   4. paddle

e. _____ ping pong   5. mallet

f. _____ polo   6. hockey stick

g. _____ fencing   7. bat

168

FACT/OPINION QUESTIONS

A *fact* is a statement that can be proven to be true or false. An *opinion* is a belief. A belief cannot be proven.

Look at the question below:

The United States did not pass the 19th Amendment, which gave women the right to vote, until 1920 because a) men still wanted women at home to cook and raise families b) women were not politically wise enough c) in those times women were not as intelligent as men d) it took over forty years for enough states to pass the 19th Amendment.

Although you might agree with some of the first three choices, they are really *opinions* and not *facts*. Usually true/false, multiple choice and short answer questions are looking for *facts* and not *opinions*.

Another kind of question asks you to identify statements as *fact* or *opinion*. It is important to know that opinions are not wrong. Opinions can be supported by facts.

Tips for finding facts

1. Facts usually explain who, what, where, or why.

2. Facts can be found in a reference book such as a dictionary, an encyclopedia, an atlas, and so on.

3. Facts are either true or false.

4. The following words are usually *not* found in factual statements.

should	may be	could have been
if	should be	probably

EXERCISE IX

Directions: Read the statements below. Decide whether they are facts or opinions. Write an
O before the statements that are opinions and an F before the statements that
are facts.

_____ 1. Children should be seen and not heard.

_____ 2. The United States had thirteen original states.

_____ 3. Dancers have a deep appreciation for music.

_____ 4. George Washington was an officer in the Continental Army.

_____ 5. The United States could have been the first country in outer space if more money
were given to space exploration in the 1950's.

_____ 6. Abraham Lincoln walked three miles to school.

_____ 7. The earth will probably have a significant climate change in the next ten years.

_____ 8. All people should have a right to equal education.

170

UNIT XV SUMMARY: STUDYING AND TEST TAKING

Your *study environment* can have a lot to do with how well you learn. Find out what kind of study environment works best for you. Then do your studying in that kind of environment.

Also try to understand how you learn the best, your *learning style*. When you study, use the ways that best help you to learn.

When you understand how different kinds of questions work, you can often do better on tests.

1. True/false questions

   If the answer is only partly false, mark it false. Watch out for "key words" like *always, never,* or *only.* These words can help you decide whether a statement is true or false.

2. Multiple choice questions

   Read the question, and see if you know the answer before you look at the choices. Then read all the choices, and pick the *best* answer. If you're not sure about the answer, cross out the choices that are wrong. Then choose the best remaining answer. Make a good guess!

3. Short answer questions

   Read the statement carefully. If you don't know the exact answer, write down the best answer you can think of.

4. Matching questions

   Match the items you know first. Then cross them out. Make a good guess about the remaining items.

5. Fact/opinion

   It is important to be able to tell fact from opinion. Multiple choice questions and true/false questions are usually looking for facts and not opinions. You can recognize facts as short bits of information that you can locate in a reference book. There are also "key words" that help you decide what are not facts, such as *should be, probably,* and *may be.*

171

PLEASE NOTE: In this unit, we have used the term "good guess" in presenting methods for answering multiple choice, matching, and short answer questions. In discussing with your students what a "good guess" is, we suggest that you introduce them to the concept of "informed guess," that is, a guess based on whatever usable knowledge you have about a question. Suggest to your students that they will want to make "informed guesses" when they need to guess. Also, you may want to remind them that if they have no basis for making an "informed guess," they will want to guess anyway, unless guessing is penalized.

ANSWERS FOR EXERCISED IN UNIT XV

Page 163: Exercise III

1. George Washington
2. general in the Revolution
3. 1797
4. Declaration of Independence
5. Thomas Jefferson
6. scientist farmer
7. 1807
8. Democratic Republican
9. Constitution
10. Dolly
11. 9
12. James Monroe
13. Revolution
14. Monroe

Page 165: Exercise V

1. F
2. F
3. T
4. F
5. F
6. T

Page 166: Exercise VI

1. D
2. D
3. C
4. B

Page 167: Exercise VII

1. three
2. John Quincy Adams
3. liquid
4. C.S. Lewis
5. Canada   Mexico

Page 168: Exercise VIII

a. 7
b. 1
c. 2
d. 6
e. 4
f. 5
g. 3

Page 170: Exercise IX

1. O
2. F
3. O
4. F
5. O
6. F
7. O
8. O

ADDITIONAL SUGGESTIONS

1. The exercises in the first part of this unit offer your students only a beginning toward gaining an understanding of their learning style and of the kind of environment in which they learn best. We suggest that you create other activities of this kind and involve your students in an ongoing experience of discovering more about their learning styles.

2. If you use other kinds of questions on your tests, involve your students in exercises like the ones in this unit, so they can develop "testwiseness" in relation to the kinds of questions that you use.

3. Ask your students to think about what questions might be on a test while they are preparing for the test. Announce a test for a specific day. Then ask your students to write some questions that they think might be asked on the test. Have the students hand in their questions before the test. Then give the test. After you've corrected the test and gone over it with your students, discuss the questions that they wrote.

    You can teach your students to use this self-questioning technique as a way of studying for a test.

4. Since much of the studying for school work is expected to take place at home, you will want to enlist the help of parents. Create a hand-out for parents such as the one that follows.

WAYS YOU CAN HELP YOUR CHILD STUDY

WHERE: Your child doesn't need an elaborate set-up. The kitchen table is a fine spot for studying. However, your child does need a spot that is fairly quiet and out of the mainstream of the family business.

WHEN: It is often best for a family to designate a certain time for studying, a time when everyone can agree to turn off the television and keep radios and CD players on low volume. For some families the hour after dinner is best. Some early risers may find the morning the most peaceful time for studying. It is probably best to avoid the times directly before bed and directly after school as these are necessary "unwinding" periods.

Whatever time your family chooses, remember that it is the repeated routine that creates a good atmosphere for studying. Also, since middle school age children require extra energy for their busy school days, it is helpful if an early bedtime is part of their routine.

MATERIALS: A shoe box can store rulers, pencils, pens, a small stapler, and any other items necessary for your child. It is probably a good idea if the rest of the family doesn't borrow items from this box.

Computers have become a common tool for school work. Your child can use a computer for writing, research, and organization. If you have a computer at home, you'll want to be sure that your child has enough use of it for school purposes. If you don't have a computer at home, you will want to arrange for your child to use a computer at school or at a library.

Reference books, such as dictionaries, atlases, and encyclopedias, can also be kept in a special spot so they are easily available to the child. Reference books are usually available on a sign-out basis from school, so no child need go without materials needed for a special assignment. You can also provide these kind of reference materials for your child by obtaining these tools in their software versions and/or gaining access to them through the Internet.

Since each of your child's teachers requires a notebook, you might check periodically to see that these notebooks are coming home and are kept updated.

JUST A FOOTNOTE . . . Ask to see your child's work. Talk about school with him or her. Discuss specific things. For instance, instead of asking how school went today, ask: How do you like using microscopes? What are you writing about? What books are you reading? Do you find fractions difficult? What kind of governments are you learning about?